Junior Golf

In

Pictures

The Junior Golfer's Handbook

Jon Paschetto

Junior Golf in Pictures

by

Jon Paschetto

eBook ISBN: 978-0-9887163-0-8

Print ISBN: 978-0-615-72238-2

Library of Congress Control Number: 2012921683

First edition: November 2012

P. Paschetto & Son, Publishers

Dedicated to all the parents who give their children a chance to play golf. And to all the adventurous young juniors who enthusiastically embrace the game.

Especially for PEP and Eileen

Dear Junior Golfer,

I hope you enjoy using this book to learn the game of golf. It is written especially for juniors, both girls and boys.

I have included lots of pictures to help you learn. Use the pictures and the text together to learn different parts of the game. I think this will help you learn the game faster and more easily because you can do it at your own pace without the need for your parents or friends to assist you all of the time.

To play golf well you will need to learn to play six different shots. These six shots are:

- Putting
- Chipping
- Pitching
- Sand shots
- Hitting the driver off a tee
- Hitting shots off the ground

I will show you the basic way to play each of these shots and when to use them when playing on the course.

You will learn many other basics of golf such as the basic rules, how to keep score, golf course etiquette and care, safety, and about many types of equipment. I will also show you some practice drills and exercises, tell you about competing and much more to help you maintain an active interest and learn skills you can use for years to come.

I wrote this book to help get you started learning and playing golf. Every good golfer needs help from others who are good teachers of the game. After a while if you decide to be serious about playing golf you should take some lessons from a PGA professional as they are the most qualified to help you.

Happy golfing,
Jon Paschetto, PGA

Atlanta, Georgia, USA

TABLE OF CONTENTS

SOME THINGS YOU SHOULD KNOW

Golf is one of the oldest sports

Golf is one of the oldest sports played with a history over 600 years. Other popular sports such as baseball, football, and basketball are all much younger sports. There is always fun stuff to learn about the old days in the sport. For instance, the earliest golf clubs were made with wooden shafts, wood or metal club heads and with leather grips. Some of the earliest golf balls were made of strips of leather sewn together and then stuffed with feathers. These early clubs didn't hit the old style ball near as far as they can fly using today's modern balls and clubs.

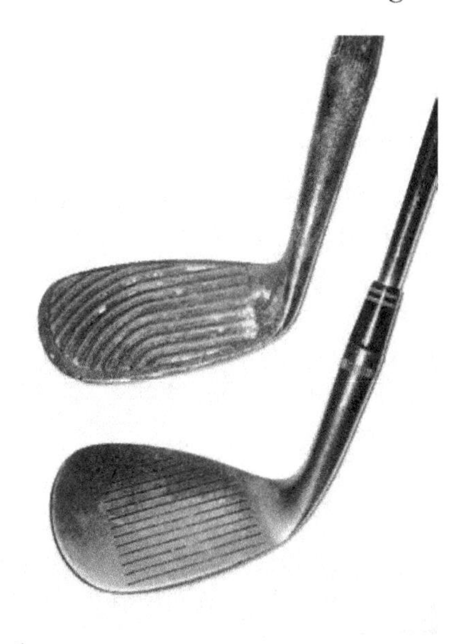

The old club on the top in this picture is from the year 1900 and is completely handmade. It has a wooden shaft, leather grip, very large, deep and inconsistent grooves (lines) on the clubface and a forged steel head.

The modern day club on the bottom is from the year 2011 and also has a forged steel club head, but with a steel shaft and rubber grip. The grooves are all made exactly the same by a computer-milling machine. This modern club is much stronger than the wooden shafted club and less likely to break.

So it is always fun to compare and study the history of the game through the years, whether it is about early equipment, old golf courses, or old day players of the game. With such a long history there is always something new to learn about golf. If you go to a library or use Google on the computer then you can learn more about golf history.

Golf courses

The neat thing about golf is that no two golf courses or golf holes are exactly the same. Playing golf will take you to some spectacular places. Enjoying the spectacular scenery and challenges in different parts of the world is a fun part of playing golf.

Golf courses can be built just about anywhere in the world - along oceans, wetlands, deserts, plains or in the mountains. Each course will have its own set of different challenges such as high winds when near the ocean, or rugged, uneven terrain when in the mountains.

The TPC Stadium course in Sawgrass, Florida even has an island green that is completely surrounded by water. The player must hit the ball well into the air to carry over the water and then hope it stays on the green once its lands. Even the best professionals sometimes have trouble and will hit a ball in the water, especially if it is a really windy when they are playing.

A golf course is also a great habitat for a lot of different animals and wildlife. Depending where you play you will see lots of different wildlife such as different birds, deer, elk, moose, fox, turtles, snakes, dolphins, alligators and even whales! It is fun to take a camera while you play to take pictures of the different wildlife you might see along the way.

Always be careful to keep a safe distance from all wildlife and never approach any wild animal. If your ball ends up too close to a wild animal, the rules allow you to drop another ball a safe distance away without any penalty. Keep an eye out for lots of great wildlife while you play!

Overall goal of the game

The overall goal of the game is to get the ball in the hole in as few "strokes" as possible.

You make a "stroke" when you swing at the ball, whether you hit it or not!

"Penalty strokes" are another part of any score you make for a hole. Most of the time you will not have any penalty strokes to add to your score, but if you hit the ball 'out of bounds', lose a ball, or hit into certain hazards, you must add a penalty stroke to your score for that hole.

Golf is a game of distance, direction & strategy

Distance: Golfers are able to hit a ball much farther than in any other sport. The longest hitters in golf can now drive a golf ball over 450 yards, the distance of four and a half football fields.

Baseball is another sport in which a player can hit a ball a long distance, but the longest home runs in baseball are less than half the distance of a long drive in golf. Hitting a golf ball really far is just one fun part of learning and playing golf.

Direction: In addition to being able to hit your golf shots to specific distances you must also have good direction control. You always want to hit your ball to where you are aiming and not too far to the left or right of where you aim.

Not being able to control direction and distance will usually put your ball in one of the hazards you are trying to avoid.

Strategy: Golf is a game of strategy and hitting correct shots. You need to be able to position your ball through the course by hitting shots of different distances to different landing areas so as to avoid the various obstacles along the way and, thereby, hole your ball in the fewest strokes.

Some obstacles to avoid on a golf course are sand bunkers and water hazards, which include rivers, streams, ponds, lakes, and oceans. Also to be avoided are trees, rough (long grass), mounds, severe slopes, waste areas and environmentally protected areas.

The diagram of a "dog leg" hole on page 242 shows some of these trouble areas.

Good players swing with tempo and balance

To be a successful golfer you must learn to begin every shot with a good address position and then achieve good balance and tempo for each swing.

We keep score

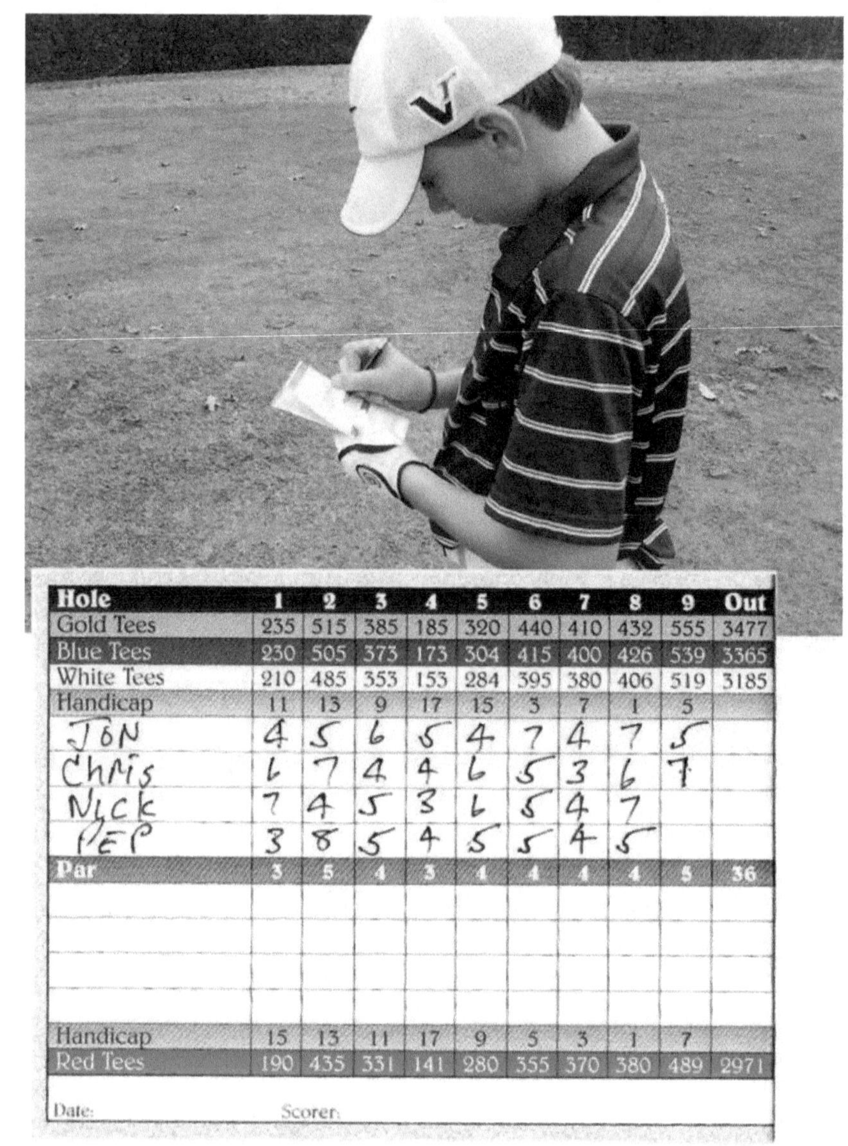

Hole	1	2	3	4	5	6	7	8	9	Out
Gold Tees	235	515	385	185	320	440	410	432	555	3477
Blue Tees	230	505	373	173	304	415	400	426	539	3365
White Tees	210	485	353	153	284	395	380	406	519	3185
Handicap	11	13	9	17	15	3	7	1	5	
JON	4	5	6	5	4	7	4	7	5	
Chris	6	7	4	4	6	5	3	6	7	
Nick	7	4	5	3	6	5	4	7		
PEP	3	8	5	4	5	5	4	5		
Par	3	5	4	3	4	4	4	4	5	36
Handicap	15	13	11	17	9	5	3	1	7	
Red Tees	190	435	331	141	280	355	370	380	489	2971

Date: Scorer:

You must add up the total of all your strokes each time you finish playing a hole. On this scorecard, the number in the green row labeled "Par" is the number (or fewer) of strokes players should strive to make when playing that hole.

Golfers try to avoid trouble

Even though a golf course has many "safe" areas such as the tees, fairways and greens, there are obstacles such as water, sand, trees, tall grass (rough), awkward mounds, and hills that you must try to avoid.

Each time your ball hits one of the obstacles you will have a more difficult time getting a good score for a hole. Part of the strategy of playing golf is to avoid these obstacles as you move your ball from the starting point of the teeing ground all the way onto the green where the hole is located.

It is always fun to play a new course as every golf course is different and offers its own special challenges and scenery.

Golfers play by the rules

Another goal when playing golf is to play within the rules. Every golfer plays by the same set of rules. When a rule is broken, most times by accident, a penalty stroke or two is added to the score for that hole.

For example if you are trying to carry your shot over water and your ball lands in the water, you must play another shot from behind the water and add a penalty stroke to your score.

You should carry a book of rules with you and learn them every chance you get.

Safety is important

Golf safety is a very important part of the sport. Juniors just beginning the game should always have an adult watching and helping them to play safely. We want to have fun playing golf, but this won't happen if anyone gets hurt on the course. Here is a list of safety concerns:

- Make sure there are no people within 15 feet of you before you start swinging your golf club.
- Do not walk near people that are swinging a club.
- Never let go of a golf club while you swing.
- Do not take practice swings (swinging without a ball) towards people, which could hit dirt at them or hit them with the club.
- Make sure all people are well out of range of your target area and the areas to the left and right of your target.
- You must quickly and loudly yell "Fore!" if your golf shot is flying towards people and could possibly hit them.
- You must quickly duck down low and cover your head with your arms when you hear someone else yell "Fore!".
- Never sit in a golf cart without an adult present. Do not touch the pedals or the cart might start to move.
- Never stand directly in front or behind a golf cart as it could start rolling.
- Wear a hat, light clothing, sunscreen and drink plenty of water on hot days. Get out of the sun and go indoors if you don't feel well from the heat.
- Immediately seek shelter indoors when lightning and thunder are threatening.
- Always look out for and avoid fire ants (looks like a small pile of sand) while walking through the course.

When to yell fore!

If your ball is traveling toward people you must loudly yell "Fore!!" to give them a fore warning to take cover from an incoming ball.

Golfers know when to stop playing

Never play in bad weather with lightning. Always seek safety indoors when lightning is coming.

Many times you will be able to go back out after the storm passes.

Golf is played in almost all kinds of weather

Bad weather such as wind, cold and rain will add extra challenges to playing golf holes. Many of the pictures in this book were taken during the "off season" of winter when the weather is cold and the grass is 'dormant'.

It is harder to make good scores under these conditions, but it is still fun to play golf.

Golfers are courteous

It is also important to play with good etiquette (proper manners). Don't ruin other players' enjoyment of their game by making distracting noises and movement such as talking, swinging, or walking while they are playing their turn.

Remember; be quiet, be still, stand out of the way.

Golfers take care of the course

You should take good care of the golf course so others can enjoy the same nice conditions that you were able to enjoy while you played.

Rake the bunker after you play out of one. Fix ball marks and divots when you make them.

Golf is a game for a lifetime

You will have fun playing golf at all ages. It is a great game to play with your family. You can have fun and enjoy playing golf with your brothers, sisters, parents, aunts, uncles, grandparents, girl friend, boy friend, and even great grandparents. You will make lots of new friends when you play golf.

Golf is an easy game to play - Not!

Golf is one of the most difficult sports to learn so enjoy the great challenge that it offers and don't let the game get you too upset or frustrated. Instead, try to overcome the difficulty of the game with patience and dedication.

Stick to it and never give up trying with your best effort.

If you can accomplish golf you can learn to accomplish lots of other challenges too.

Even when you are not playing your best, golf is great exercise to stay healthy

GOLF CLUBS & OTHER STUFF

Like every other sport, golf has its own type of special gear.

- Golf clubs
- Golf bag
- Golf balls
- Golf glove
- Towel
- Tees
- Ball marker
- Golf shoes
- Rule book

Don't worry. You don't have to get all of this stuff before you can start. I'm going to start you off with putting. You will only need a single club and one golf ball!

Parts of a golf club

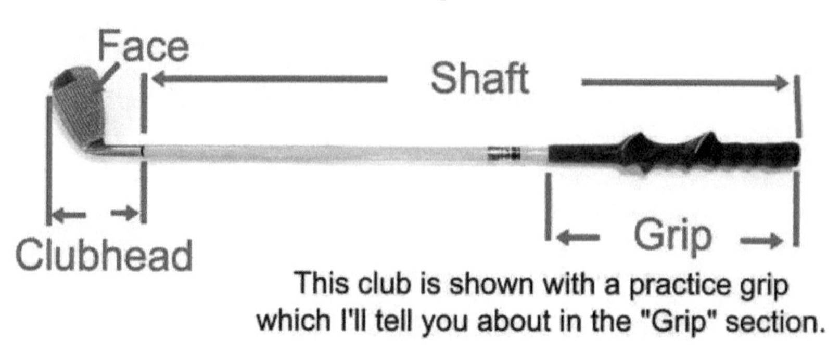

This club is shown with a practice grip which I'll tell you about in the "Grip" section.

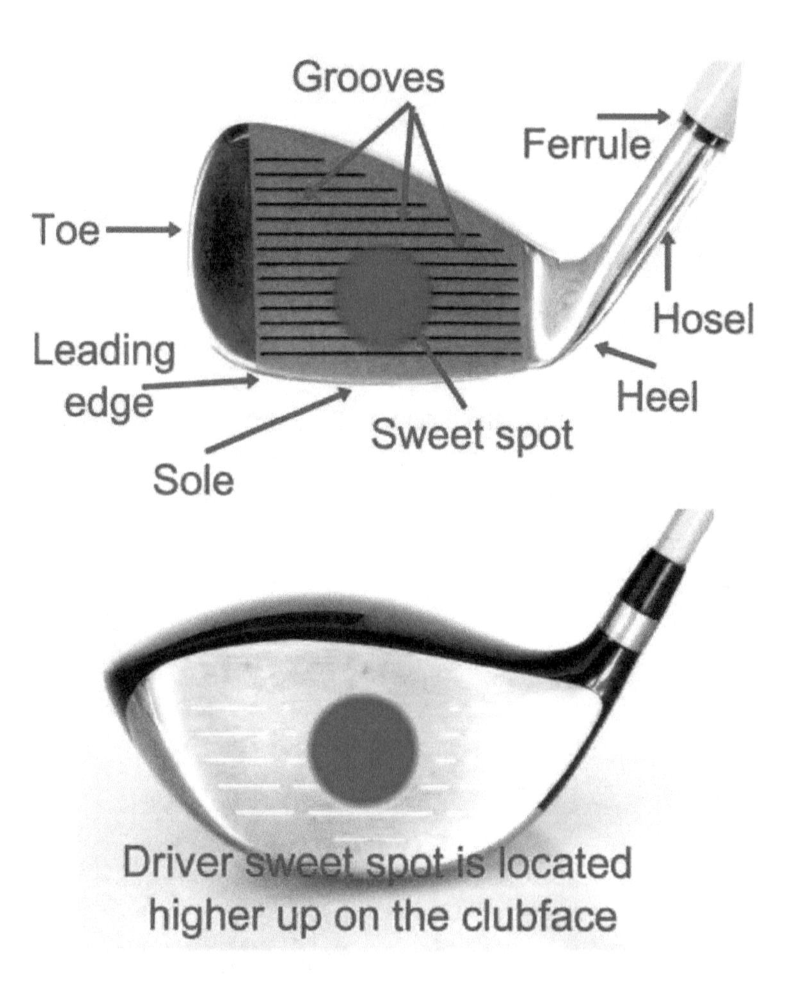

Golf clubs and a golf bag

The best way for juniors age 3 up to age 11 to get started is to buy a matched junior set of golf clubs. It will have 7 or 8 clubs in the set and also include a golf bag.

Why you need different clubs

The rules allow you to play with up to 14 clubs in your golf bag. Why do golfers have so many different clubs?

The basic answer is that each club is designed to go a different distance and whatever distance you need to hit your ball will determine which club you choose to play your shot.

A junior set of clubs

The driver hits the ball the longest distance off the tee. Unless you are hitting the ball 180-200 yards with your driver you won't need 14 clubs as a beginning junior.

You will only need 6-9 clubs to go all the different distances you will experience on the course.

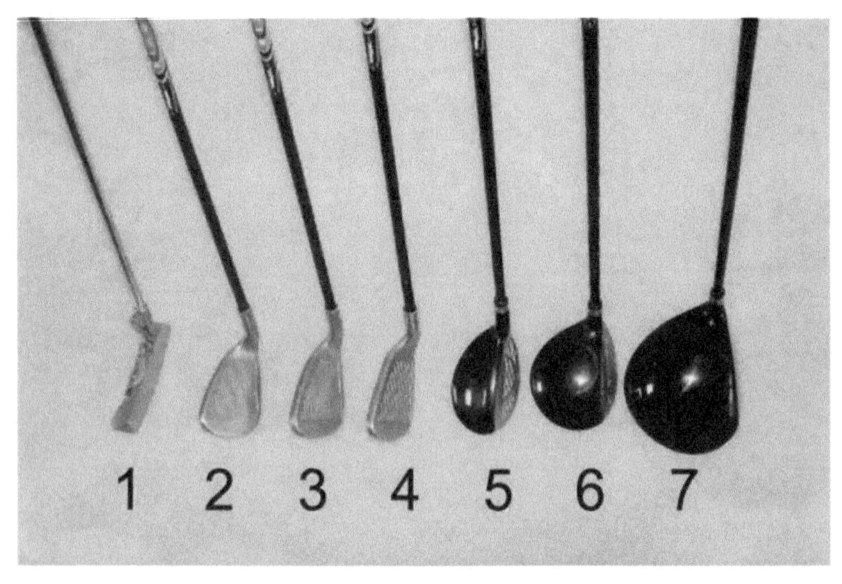

A good junior set will include a: 1) putter, 2) sand wedge, 3) nine iron, 4) seven iron, 5) 5-hybrid, 6) fairway club and 7) driver. A matched set will give you the proper clubs for all the different distances and shots you need to hit.

Junior golf sets come in many different lengths. When you go to buy a junior set it will tell you on the box what size player, according to height, the junior clubs are designed for. Pay close attention to these measurements and purchase a set for your specific height.

Play with the correct clubs

Having properly fit clubs is important for juniors. If you are a junior under the age of 11 you will only need a complete set of about 8 clubs to play all of your shots.

Based on your height, the club manufacturing companies will produce clubs with the correct grip size, shaft flex, club length, overall club weight, and proper lofts and lie angles between clubs. Ping and U.S. Kids Golf are two of the best companies for junior club sets.

Fitting by a PGA Professional

The most important factor when shopping for junior clubs is to get the proper length clubs for your specific height.

Golf clubs that are too long or too short for your height will make hitting good golf shots much more difficult.

If you can go to a golf course pro shop and have a PGA Professional help fit you to the proper length it will help ensure that you get the right size.

Getting measured for a proper fit.

When you will need 14 clubs

As you grow stronger and begin to hit the ball farther and with more power you will need a complete set of 14 clubs.

With a beginner set you would have a big distance gap between clubs if you just carry every other numbered club such as 5, 7, 9, and sand wedge.

Closing the distance gap

If you hit your 7 iron 125 yards and your 9 iron 100 yards that means you have a big distance gap of 25 yards difference between clubs. How would you hit a shot of 110-115 yards with your 7 or 9 irons? You would have to try to adjust your swing.

This is when it is an advantage to get a full set of irons. An 8 iron will fill the distance gap and let you hit a 115-yard shot so you don't have to adjust your swing

You must know the distance you hit each club

As you develop and learn to play golf you will want to write down on an index card how far you hit each club so you know which club to use each time on the course.

Remember that everyone hits the ball different distances. An 80-yard distance for one player might be a nine iron and a 7 iron for another player.

Your size, strength, and technique together will determine how far you hit each club.

8 year old junior's average yardage for each club

- Driver -120-140 yards
- 3 wood – 115-130 yards
- 6 hybrid 100-115 yards
- 7 iron 90-100 yards
- 9 iron 70-90 yards
- Sand wedge – up to 70 yards.

Your distances will vary based on your size and ability

10 year old junior's average yardage for each club

- Driver- 140-170 yards
- Five wood 135-145 yards
- Hybrid 120-135 yards
- Seven iron 110-120 yards
- 9 iron 90-110 yards
- Sand wedge – up to 90 yards

Your distances will vary based on your size and ability.

12 year old junior's average yardage for each club

If you are 12 years old and can hit a driver 180-220 yards then you should consider using a full 14 club set so you can easily hit to a wider range of different distances.

- Driver -180-220 yards
- Three wood 170-185 yards
- Five Wood-160-175 yards
- Hybrid 5 –150-165 yards
- Six iron –140-155 yards
- Seven iron – 130-145 yards
- Eight iron-120-135 yards
- Nine iron- 110-125 yards
- Pitching wedge- 90-110 yards
- Sand wedge-up to 90 yards

Your distances will vary based on your size and ability

What are your averages?

- Driver -___________ yards
- Three wood - __________yards
- Five Wood-____________yards
- Hybrid -__________ yards
- Six iron -___________yards
- Seven iron – __________ yards
- Eight iron-__________yards
- Nine iron- __________ yards
- Pitching wedge- __________ yards
- Sand wedge-up to __________ yards

Knowing your averages is not easy. You must play a lot of shots with the same club and then average the distances you hit each shot.

Your averages will increase as you get stronger and you learn how to make a repeating golf swing.

Keep track of your averages with a small notebook or index card.

Some things you will need

The next few items you will need are golf balls, a golf towel, tees, ball marker, pencil, divot tool and a golf glove.

Try and get at least 15 to 20 balls to start and store them in your golf bag until you use them. You can use these balls to play and practice.

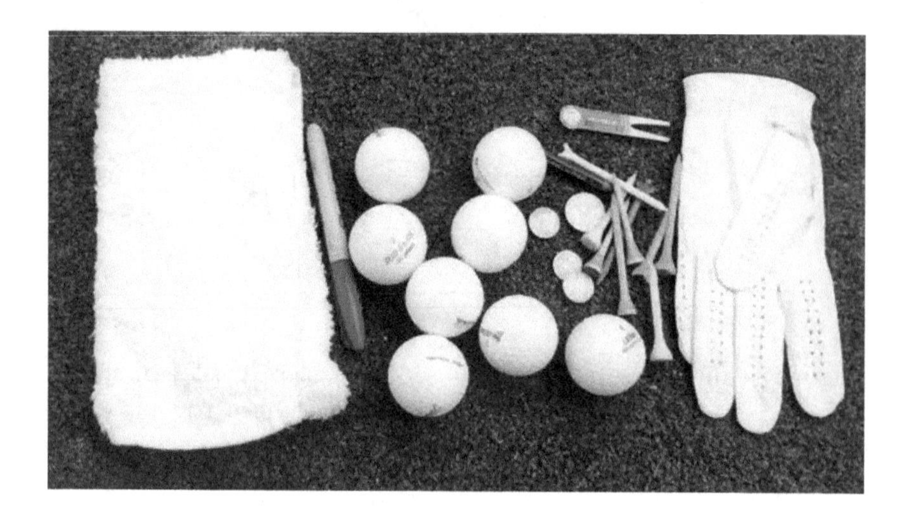

Golf tees are used to prop the ball up above the ground on each teeing area.

A golf towel will help keep your clubs clean while playing.

A golf glove is good to have as a beginner as it helps keep the club from slipping in your hands.

Pennies or other small coins can be used as ball markers.

A divot repair tool so you can repair ball marks on the green.

A marker pen is handy to mark your golf balls so they are easy to identify.

Golf safety quiz

Cover up this page with a sheet of paper. See how many of the safety concerns on page 9 you can remember, in any order, without looking. Here's a hint. There are eleven of them.

- Make sure there are no people within 15 feet of you before you start swinging your golf club.
- Do not walk near people that are swinging a club.
- Never let go of a golf club while you swing.
- Do not take practice swings (swinging without a ball) towards people, which could hit dirt at them or hit them with the club.
- Make sure all people are well out of range of your target area and the areas to the left and right of your target.
- You must quickly and loudly yell "Fore!" if your golf shot is flying towards people and could possibly hit them.
- You must quickly duck down low and cover your head with your arms when you hear someone else yell "Fore!".
- Never sit in a golf cart without an adult present. Do not touch the pedals or the cart might start to move.
- Never stand directly in front or behind a golf cart as it could start rolling.
- Wear a hat, light clothing, sunscreen and drink plenty of water on hot days. Get out of the sun and go indoors if you don't feel well from the heat.
- Immediately seek shelter indoors when lightning and thunder are threatening.
- Always look out for and avoid fire ants (looks like a small pile of sand) while walking through the course.

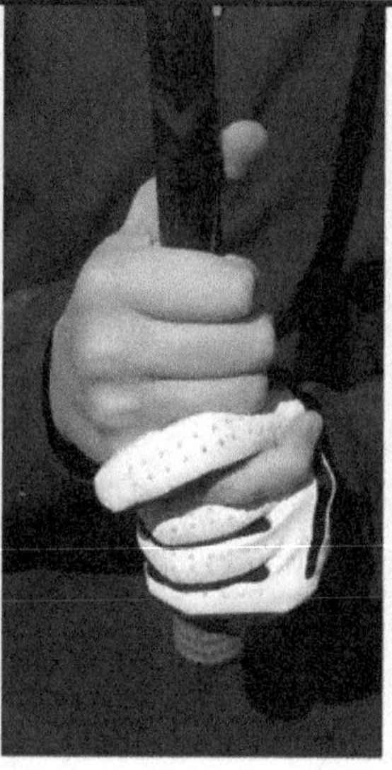

Lesson 1
PUTTING

LESSON 1 - PUTTING

What you will need.

- A putter
- A golf ball
- A putting cup
- Some places to practice. An indoor carpeted area and a practice green at a golf course.

Putting, one key to low scores

We're going to start with putting because you can get started on it right away with only one club and a ball. You can practice indoors all year around on a smooth carpet.

Putting will count for almost half of your score when you play. A good putter will have a better score than a poor putter every time!

So let's find a putter and a few golf balls and get you started on the way to becoming a good putter.

Choosing a putter

Putters come in all different shapes, sizes, and materials. It is fun to try lots of different putters. You will discover that there are slight differences in their performance and feel.

In choosing a putter you will first want a putter that fits your size.

Next, use a putter that you like the look and feel of and that aligns easily to the target.

Most importantly choose the putter that works the best for you. You will know when you find a putter that you like.

See Chris in this golf store picture. He is surrounded by hundreds of different putters and is trying and comparing them.

Putting basics

Putting is an extremely fun and challenging part of golf. Putting is rolling the ball on the putting green and into the hole using the flat-faced club called the putter.

Each time you hit the ball with your putter it is called a stroke or a putt.

Your goal when putting

Your goal when putting is to take just one or two putts in getting the ball into the hole on each green. When you are putting and take 3, 4, 5 or more putts on each green it makes your score go up quickly.

The nice thing about putting is that kids can putt every bit as well as adults.

Good putting doesn't depend on strength or size

Putting doesn't require that you be super tall or have super strength. Anybody can be a great putter once you learn to do some of the basics of putting really well.

Putt for distance

You have to be able to swing your putter back and through with good tempo to strike the ball so it goes the correct distance to the hole, or, just slightly beyond the hole if it misses.

A ball less than 18 inches past the hole is best for a missed putt.

Putt for direction

You have to be able to line up and hit your putt in the correct direction so if it misses the hole the ball stops near the hole.

Use your imagination

Putting greens are not flat and level. The ball does not always roll straight. In fact, most times it rolls along a curved path because of the slope and hilliness of the green.

Putting well requires that you have a good imagination. You have to be able to imagine the path the ball will roll before hitting it.

Most kids have a great imagination so beginning golf at a young age is a big advantage to becoming a good player.

You also need to use your imagination to predict how hard to hit your putt to make the ball go the correct distance to the hole. Uphill requires a slightly bigger putting stroke and downhill a slightly smaller stroke.

As the ball rolls along the green the slopes will make the ball curve left or right so you do not always aim directly at the center of the hole when you putt. Imagination will help you decide where to aim.

The curved path is called the 'break'. Almost all putts have some break to them.

"Read' the break

The boy pictured is getting down low behind his ball before he putts. He is looking toward the hole and trying to predict how the slopes will affect his ball as it rolls towards the hole. The side slopes will make his ball move left or right and the up and down slopes will slow or speed up his putt.

Play the break

To play the break you have to aim indirectly (not exactly at the hole) but to the left or right of the hole and let the slope bring the ball toward the hole.

Your putting grip

The grip for putting is much different than the full swing grip. In making this grip we want to place our hands close together, but with our thumbs going straight down the shaft on the flat part of the golf grip.

This grip also places the shaft across our palms for each hand. Make this grip as shown in these pictures with your hands close together and thumbs straight down the shaft.

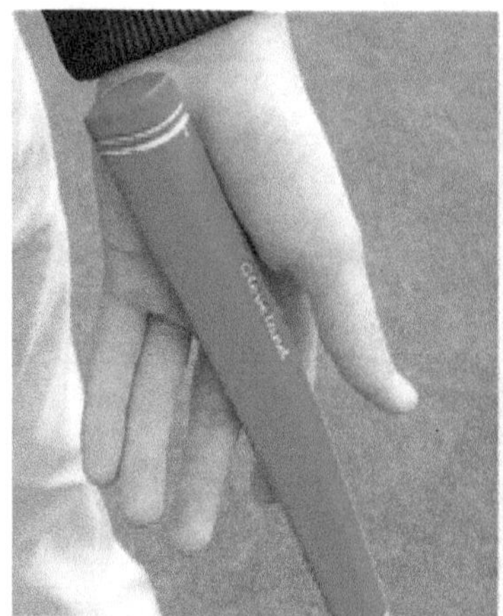

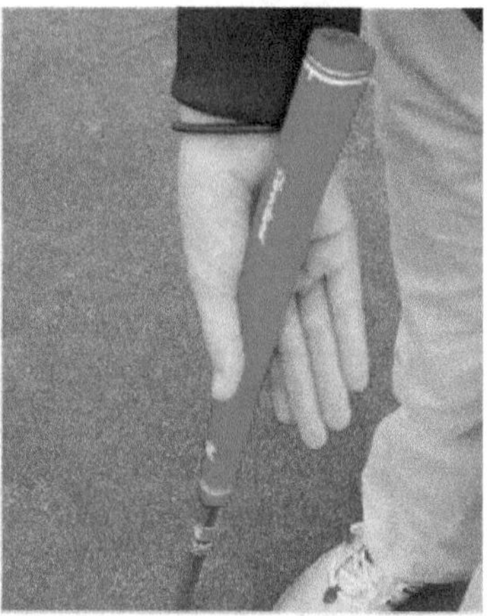

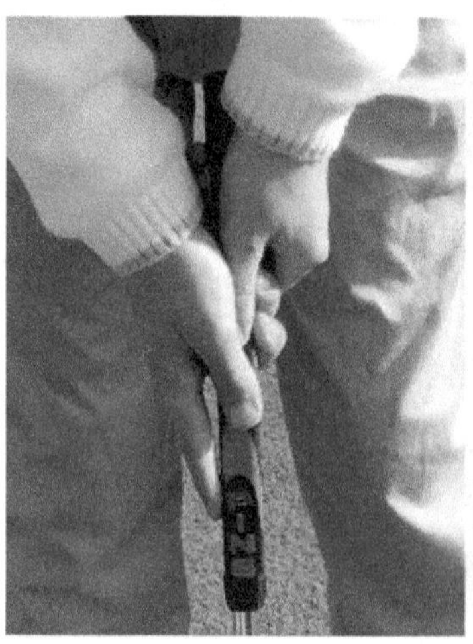

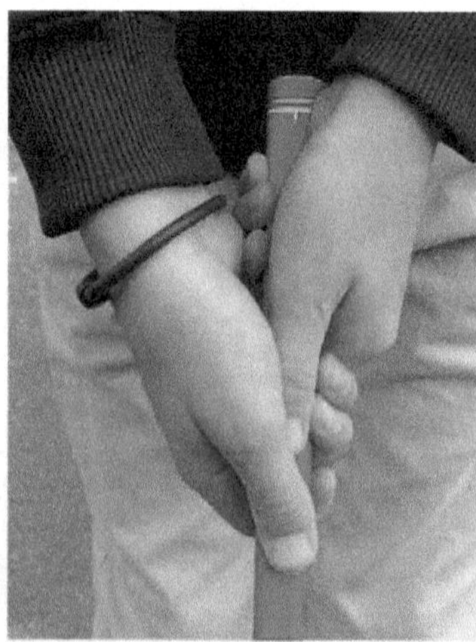

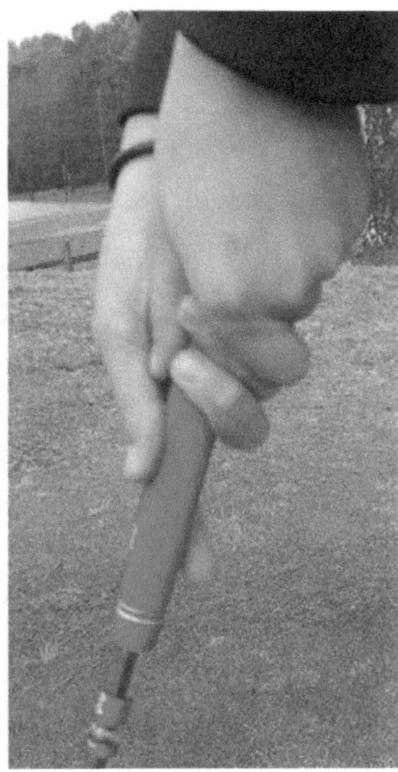

This is called a reverse overlap grip and a wonderful way to grip the putter and begin learning to putt.

Just place your left index finger over your right pinky to produce the reverse overlap grip.

Some players try this grip with their right index finger down the shaft. Try it both ways to see which way works best for you.

Notice to lefties

We don't have enough room to show both left hand and right hand pictures. They are exactly the same, but in reverse. You can see how a left hand grip, stance, swing, etc. looks by holding the picture up to a mirror. This is true for all of the pictures in this book.

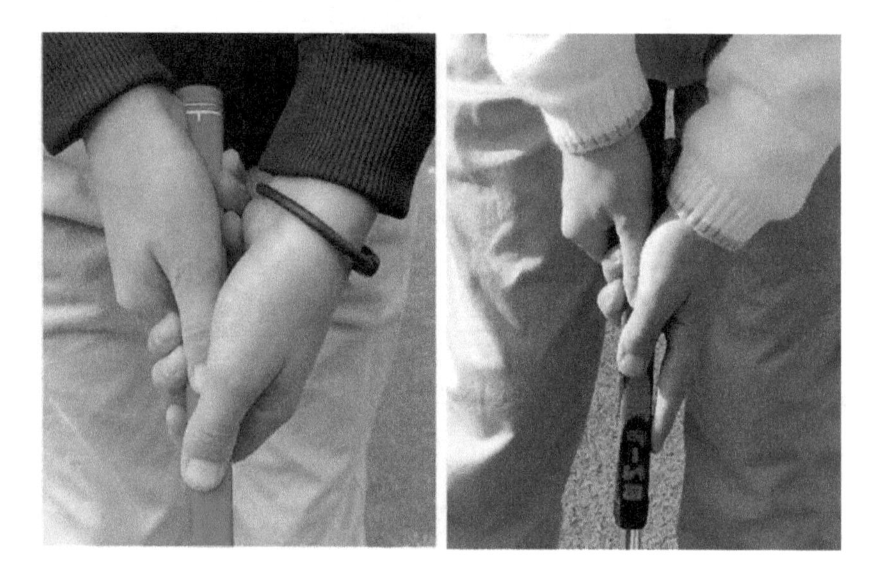

Mirror image showing left handed putting grip.

Your putting stance

Once you achieve a good grip stand with your feet together and hold the putter out in front of you with the clubface pointing exactly sideways.

Now bend from the waist and set the club down behind a ball and spread each of your feet apart a few inches.

Your eyes should be right over the ball so that if you dropped a ball from your eyes you would drop it right onto the ball on the ground. Having your eyes over the ball is a key fundamental to good putting and it will help you to properly line up your putts.

How to aim the putter

Many balls have a line printed on them to help you line up your putter.

#1. The ball is lined up to the target line for a straight putt.

#2. The putter is lined up with the target line using the line on the ball as a helper.

#3. The ball and the putter are lined up ready to make the putt.

Your putting stroke

A great way to putt is to use only your arms and shoulders in a back and forth motion with a smooth tempo like a grandfather clock pendulum that swings gently back and forth.

No wrist hinging

The best putters don't have much wrist movement while they make their putting stroke. Their wrists don't 'hinge' back and forth when they swing their arms and shoulders back and forth.

Distance control

To help you get good distance control on your putts make your putting stroke with a nice smooth back and forth motion. Try not to swing the putter too fast or with a fast jerky back and forth motion.

Smooth tempo

Gripping the putter with a light grip pressure will help achieve smooth tempo. Think of the grandfather clock pendulum going back and forth or watching someone going back and forth on a swing set. This is similar to the tempo or speed you want to copy for your putting stroke. Think about a nice tick tock gentle tempo and this will give you the best chance of controlling the distance you hit a putt.

Combine this good tempo with the length you take the putter back and forth and you will make great putts.

Small putts = small swing length.

Medium putts=medium length swing,

Long putts =longer length swing.

Try to make your backswing and follow through match up in swing length so 8 inches back swing from the ball = 8 inches past the spot of the ball in follow thru. As you swing the putter back and forth the ball will just start rolling nicely along the ground.

Putting stroke for a long putt

As the putter swings back and forth it should not hit the ground. Practice making small back and forth strokes while keeping the putter head very close to the ground without ever touching the ground.

The 'sweet spot'

In putting you always want to hit the putt in the center of the clubface also known as the "sweet spot" as marked with a line on the top of the putter. Hitting the ball any other place on the clubface will result in bad distance and direction control.

A great practice drill to help you hit the sweet spot on the putter is to use a couple of tees to create a "gate" one inch wider than the club head. Practice hitting putts through the gate and not hit the tees.

Tip for learning break.

Set up two gates to putt your ball through for a breaking putt. Put two tees 5 inches apart and five feet away from you on a putt that breaks sharply on a side hill.

Try to hit your putts so they go through the second gate and then into the hole.

Make this into a contest and try to hit 10 balls through the gate. You will have to adjust the tees to the gate to get the break just right so the ball goes through the gate and also in the hole.

The putter is swinging inside a gate too, and this helps you to hit the sweet spot each time you make your stroke. This is a great drill and will help you to learn and visualize break on future putts.

Your putting routine

When you are on the course you need a routine to go through for each putt. A routine is a series of steps you follow each time to prepare for your putt. Here is an example of a great putting routine:

Read the break

As you become a better junior player, reading the slope of the green is the first thing you should be thinking about as you walk toward and approach a green. The first thing you want to know is whether your putt is uphill or downhill in order to get good distance control for your putt. Distance control in putting is the hardest part of putting and where most juniors are easily fooled.

Juniors will sometimes have a ten-foot putt downhill and then have a twenty-foot putt coming back because they didn't realize they were going so much downhill!

The best two ways to learn the slopes are to always go to the lowest point on the green so you are looking up the slope. An uphill view always gives you the best view of the green in order to sense the slope.

The next way is to walk along the side of your putt and use your feet to sense whether you are walking uphill or downhill.

So remember, always know first whether your putt is uphill or downhill to get good distance control.

Line up the ball

Line up your ball in the direction you want to start your putt.

Practice swing

Take one or two practice swings standing to the side of your ball. A good practice swing should be exactly like the stroke you will use on the ball.

Aim your putter

Next align your putter to the line on the ball. Line up your feet parallel to the putter.

Now look at the hole then back to your ball and imagine the proper speed and line into the hole.

Make the putt

Stroke your putt and then hold the finish of your stroke.

Putting set up keys

You will find there are times you will want to use the putter from off the green instead of chipping.

Practice to improve your putting

Practice green

Here is a way to practice getting better with your putting distance control. You can do this with a friend and make it a fun competition or you can do it by yourself. Either way this will help you get better.

Place a few balls in a line every 3 feet apart at 3', 6', 9', 12', etc. Try to make these putts starting with the ball closest to the hole. Try to hit your putts so that if they miss they finish just past the hole in the area inside the 3-foot long stick placed 24 inches past the hole. Try not to hit the stick with your putts.

Your goal is to always make the ball go in the hole, but if it misses to try and get it to finish just past the hole. Then your next putt will be easier to make because it is close to the hole.

We do this drill from four different directions around the hole; north, south, west and east. This will give us an uphill, downhill and two different side hill angles to teach us speed and break.

Golf courses will vary with the speed of their greens and also the amount of slopes so it is important to use the practice green before playing to adjust to the course conditions you will be playing.

In the house

Use a piece of wood or cardboard to make a practice cup. The opening should be the size of a golf hole, which is 4 1/4 inches. This one is made out of wood, but you could use a piece of cardboard.

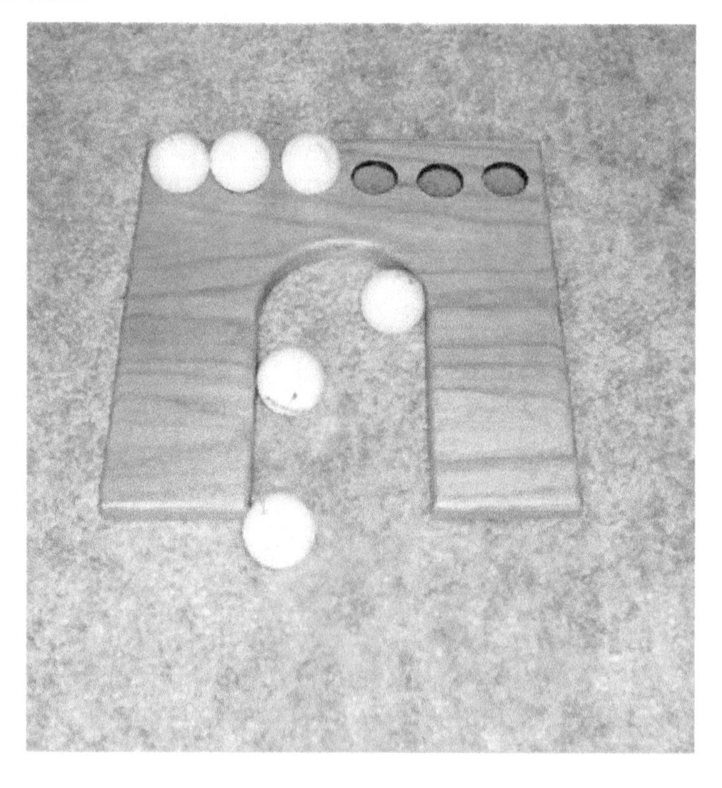

Place your putting cup on a smooth carpeted floor about 5 feet from where you will stand.

Also, there are lots of putting cups and mats for sale online and at sporting goods stores.

Practice, practice and more practice make a good putter!

Putting games

Here are a few putting games that you can do with your friends. These games are a greet way to improve your putting while also competing in fun formats with your friends.
You will always use a large practice green near the clubhouse for these games.

Basic putting contest

Decide which player will go first. That player picks a putt of any distance they like to any hole of their choosing.
Every hole is a par two. The winner of the hole always has the honor (plays first) and selects the next putt.
The game winner is the player with the lowest score after 18 holes.

Bocce putting

For 2 or 4 players

Bocce putting is a great game to play with your friends and also improves your putting skills in a fun and competitive manner. You will improve your distance and direction control just as if you were practicing to a hole, but this adds the great game of Italian Bocce into the fun of practicing. Caution: can be very addicting!! Here's how to play.

You should always use a large practice green for this game.

You need two sets of four balls each set a different color. These are the bocce balls. Each player, or team, uses four bocce balls of the same color.

A two-player team will each putt two balls.

One white ball is used and is called the jack or pallina ball.

Flip a coin to decide who will go first.

The winner of the coin toss places a tee down to mark the starting point and then putts the pallina ball to a distance of his choosing. This can be anywhere from 8 to 100 feet. Then:

1. Once the pallina comes to rest, the first player putts and tries to get his first bocce putt very close to the pallina ball.

2. Then, the first player on the other team putts his team's first bocce ball and tries to get it closer than the other player's first ball.

3. Now, the team furthest from the pallina putts again. The team furthest from the pallina ball keeps putting until they have used all four of their bocce balls. The other team then finishes putting their bocce balls.

The player, or team, that has a bocce ball nearest to the pallina ball scores one point for each ball that is closer to the pallina than their opponent's nearest ball.

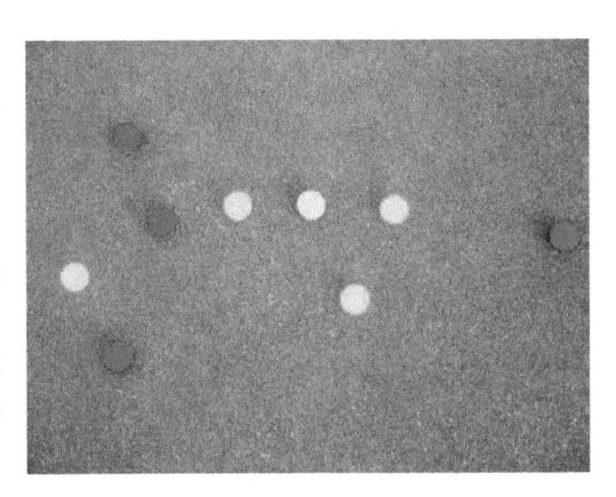

As you can see in this picture the yellow team scores three points.

Repeat 1, 2, and 3.

The player, or team, that scores 13 points first is the winner. Repeat game for even more fun!

Drawback & safety drawback

For two or more players

On a practice green, the first player picks a putt to any hole and at any distance of her choosing. Each player then putts from the same spot to the same hole.

If you miss with your first putt and your ball doesn't go in the hole you then have to move (drawback) your ball further from the hole by the length of your putter. So if your ball is 12 inches from the hole and your putter is 36 inches long, your next putt will be 48 inches. Keep putting and drawing back until the ball is in the hole.

Count your putts. The winner is the player with the lowest score. after 9 or 18 holes.

Safety drawback uses the same rules except, if you putt your ball past the hole you do not have to drawback. You can just putt the ball from where it lies.

Game of 21

21 is a point game for any number of players and the more players the better. The object is to be the first to score exactly 21 points.

The first player picks a putt of any distance to any hole of his choice. Then each player putts to that hole and one point is awarded to the player closest to the hole, or three points for each player who scores a hole in one.

You must score exactly 21 points to win. If you have 19 or 20 points and you make a hole in one, or another player knocks your ball into the hole and you go over 21, then you must subtract 5 points from your score as a penalty.

The first player to score exactly 21 points wins. Super fun!

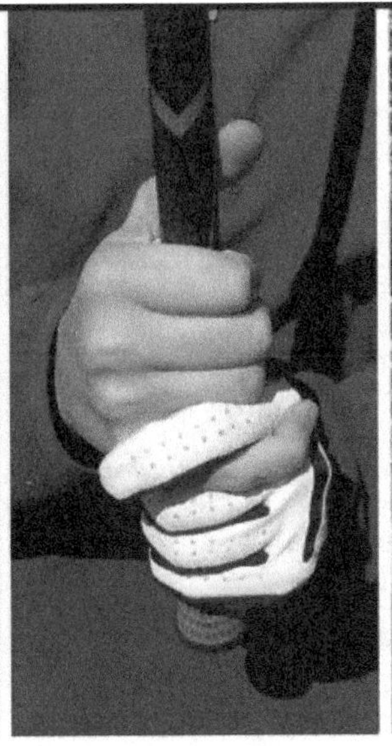

Lesson 2
GRIP

Lesson 2 - THE GRIP

The grip you use for the full swing shot is different from your putting grip.

How you position your hands on the golf club is an important fundamental of your 'set up' because it is how you connect to the club and will determine how well you will be able to control the club while you swing the club.

You want to hold the club securely so you can swing with both speed and club face control, which together will give you both distance and accuracy when the ball is struck solidly. When you play tennis or ping pong you hold the racket and paddle so you can swing them while at the same time knowing where the racket face is facing so you can return the ball back over to the opponents side.

Golf is very similar, you want to be able to swing athletically and return the clubface into the ball so you can hit the ball in the desired direction and distance.

You achieve this control by positioning your hands at the beginning of your set up to the ball and then you keep them in the same position throughout the swing. Your hands cannot come off, slide or let go from the grip once you begin swinging.

When you grip you want your hands close together with no gap between them. The left hand is higher than the right hand for a right handed junior. Your left thumb should be underneath your right palm.

Three ways to grip the club for the full swing

Overlap grip

Ten finger grip

The 10-finger grip for younger juniors (age 1-9)

Interlock grip

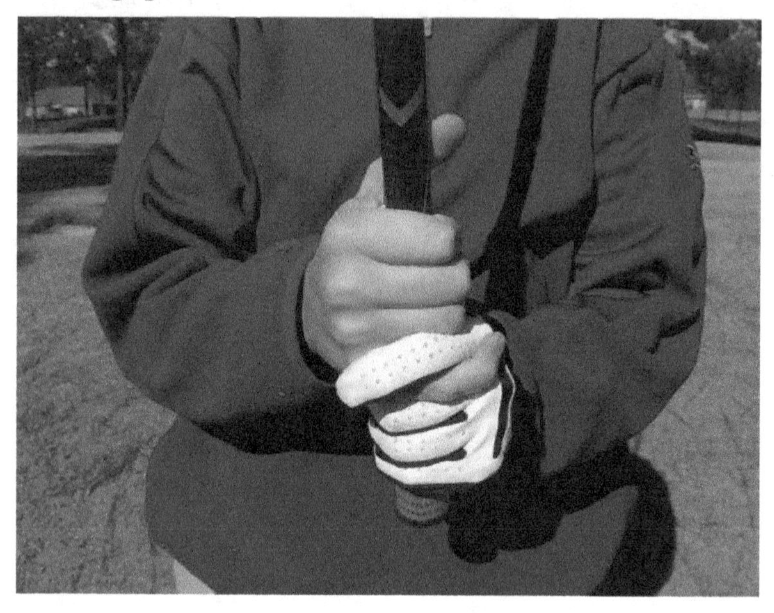

If you are 9-10 years or older I recommend you use the interlock grip.

How to achieve the interlock grip

Right hand

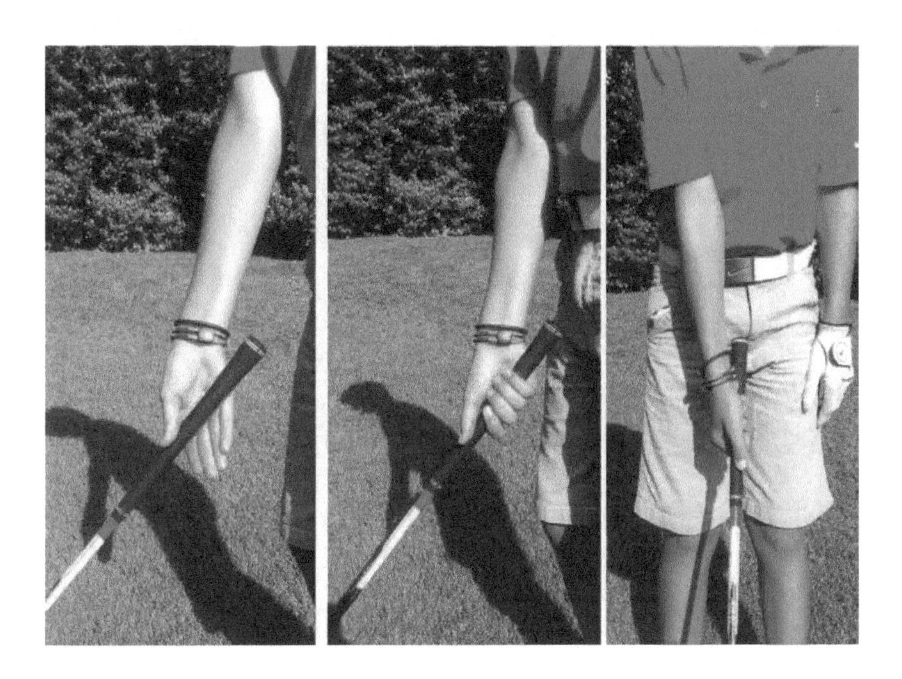

Your right hand grips the club where your fingers meet the palm of your hand. Check out the position of the thumb on top of the grip and a little to the left side of the shaft.

Left hand

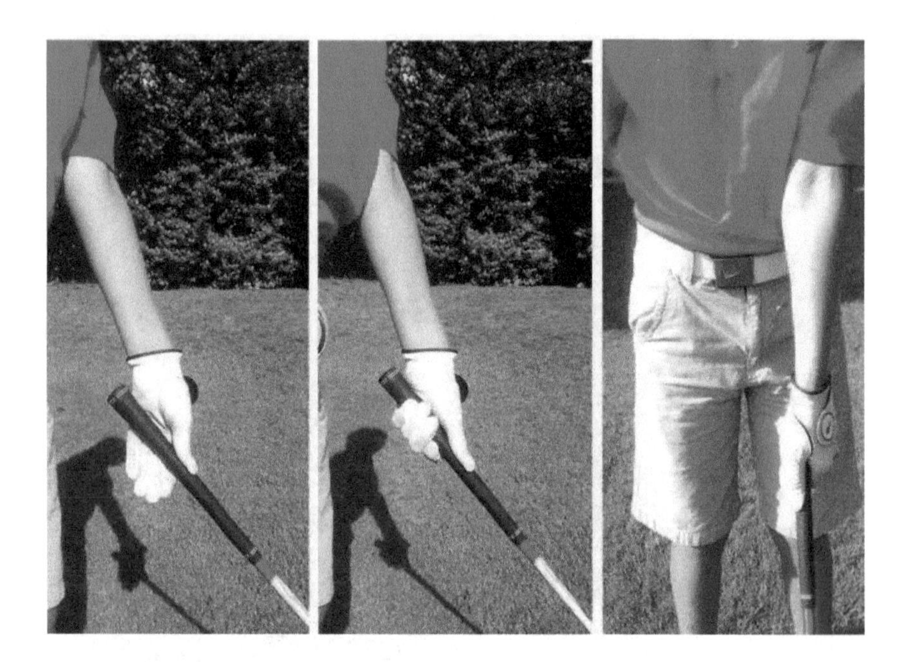

Your left hand grips the club where the fingers meet the palm of your hand.

Your thumb will be on top and a little to the right side of the shaft.

Both hands

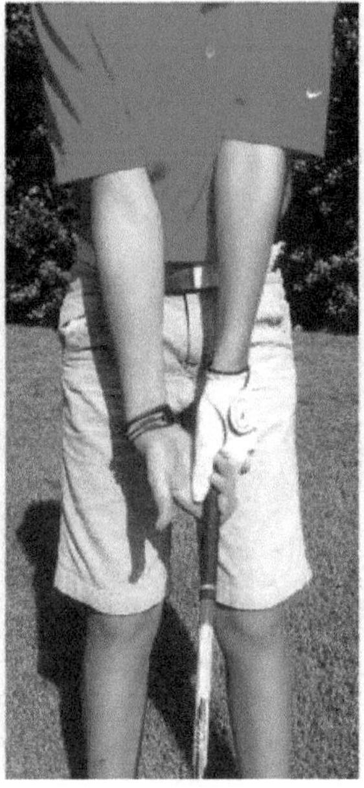
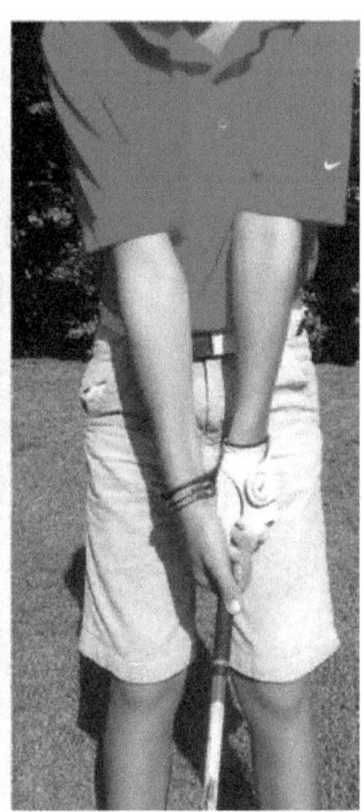

Now grip the club with both hands like this.

'Interlock' the pinky finger of your right hand with the index finger of your left hand as shown on page 64.

You should see two or three knuckles of your left hand when you place the club head on the ground and the clubface is aligned directly at the target.

This is a great grip position to begin learning golf as a junior and also the way many tour pro golfers grip the club with their left hand.

Grip check and drills

Keep a firm grip on the club

Let's imagine that your hands are glued on to the club so that as you swing the club your hands do not loosen their hold on the grip.

Don't loosen, separate your hands from the grip or let go of the club while swinging.

This is the most difficult thing to learn about gripping the club when beginning golf.

Grip strengthening drills

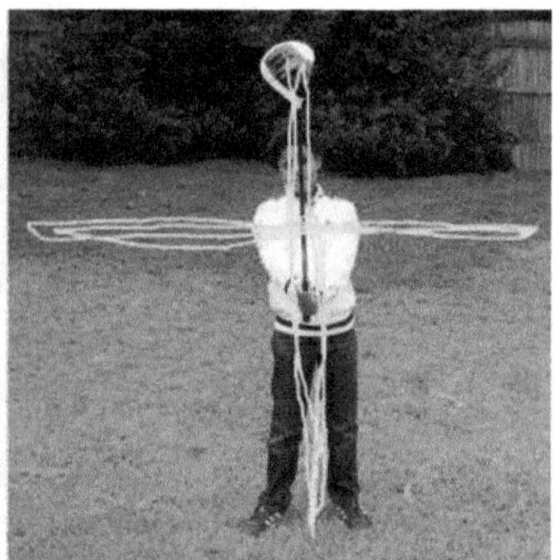

Here are two grip-strengthening drills to learn a secure and athletic grip.

Drill #1. Once you follow the directions for placement of your hands hold your club out in front of you and practice making circles in the air with the club head using your wrists.

As you make circles feel the muscles in your fingers and hands hold the club securely without coming off the grip.

Drill #2. After making circles make some up and down and then some side to side waggles.

Once you are able to do this drill slowly and still keep a good grip on the club, then try to do it with more speed without loosening your grip.

Grip training mold

A grip-training mold is a wonderful teaching aid to guide your hands into the correct grip position. These grips come in a variety of different sizes to fit your hands and also in lefty versions and can easily be purchased at a golf shop or online.

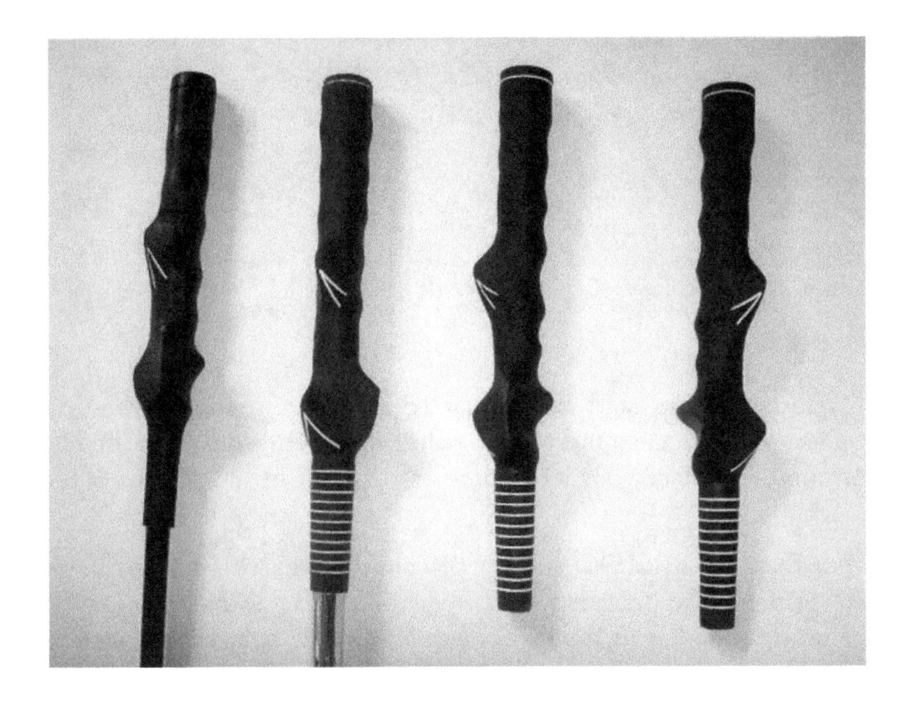

You can either add it onto the shaft of a golf club or just use it alone to practice your grip while you watch golf on television.

To use the grip start by placing your left hand against the grip where your fingers meet your palm and then wrap your fingers around and place your left thumb to the right of the painted white "V".

For the right hand also start by placing the grip where your fingers meet the palm and wrap your fingers around and have your right thumb to the left of the lower "V". Place your right index finger in the lower groove.

You can use either the ten-finger grip, the Vardon overlap or the interlock grip. The ten-finger grip is best for 5-10 year olds, and the interlock and Vardon grips best for ages eleven and up.

Practice maintaining your grip while you repeat waggling your wrists back and forth and up and down without your hands separating or coming apart, especially where the right palm is against the left thumb. Maintain a grip pressure that allows you to swing freely, but not so tight that you have a lot of tension in your hands and wrists.

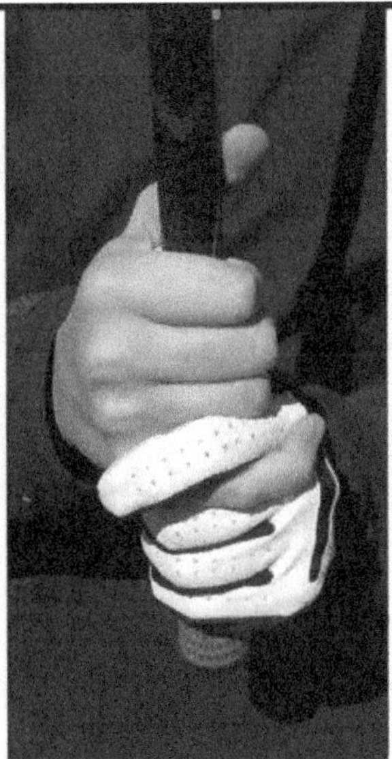

Lesson 3
SHORT GAME

Lesson 3 - The SHORT GAME

What you will need.

- Sand wedge
- Seven iron
- 10-12 golf balls
- Places to practice: Back yard. A golf course practice area. Driving range.

Chipping

Chipping is a short shot where you make a mini swing with an iron to lift the ball into the air a short distance to go over some long grass and land the ball onto the green where it can then roll easily towards the hole. A mini golf swing is only a shorter backswing and shorter follow through.

This shot is similar to making an underhanded toss with a ball to get it to finish at a target that is very close to you.

The underhand toss

Making an underhanded toss with a ball to a nearby target is a good way to get an understanding of chipping.

You will get an idea of how high or low the ball needs to be tossed and at what speed in order to get the ball to finish close to the hole for different distances.

You then try to transfer that knowledge of the speed and amount of arm swing required to go a short distance for the club you choose to chip with.

The chip shot set up

I recommend that you begin learning to chip with a 9 iron and sand wedge because most junior sets include these clubs. You don't need a big swing to go a short distance.

This is a good set up for chipping. His hands and the shaft are leaning slightly forward of the club head and ball. His feet are close together.

The chip shot swing

Chip with your arms and shoulders similar to a putting technique. Very important when chipping is to get the ball in the air when you swing through the ball.

The way to get the ball in the air is to brush the grass where it meets the ground with the sole of the club at the point where the ball is located.

Chipping around the green

Most of the time you'll want to land the ball on the green and let it roll to the hole.

Uphill chip shot

Angle your body perpendicular to the slope so you can swing the club along the slope otherwise your club will hit and stop into the hill and the ball won't go where you want it to go.

Chipping set up keys

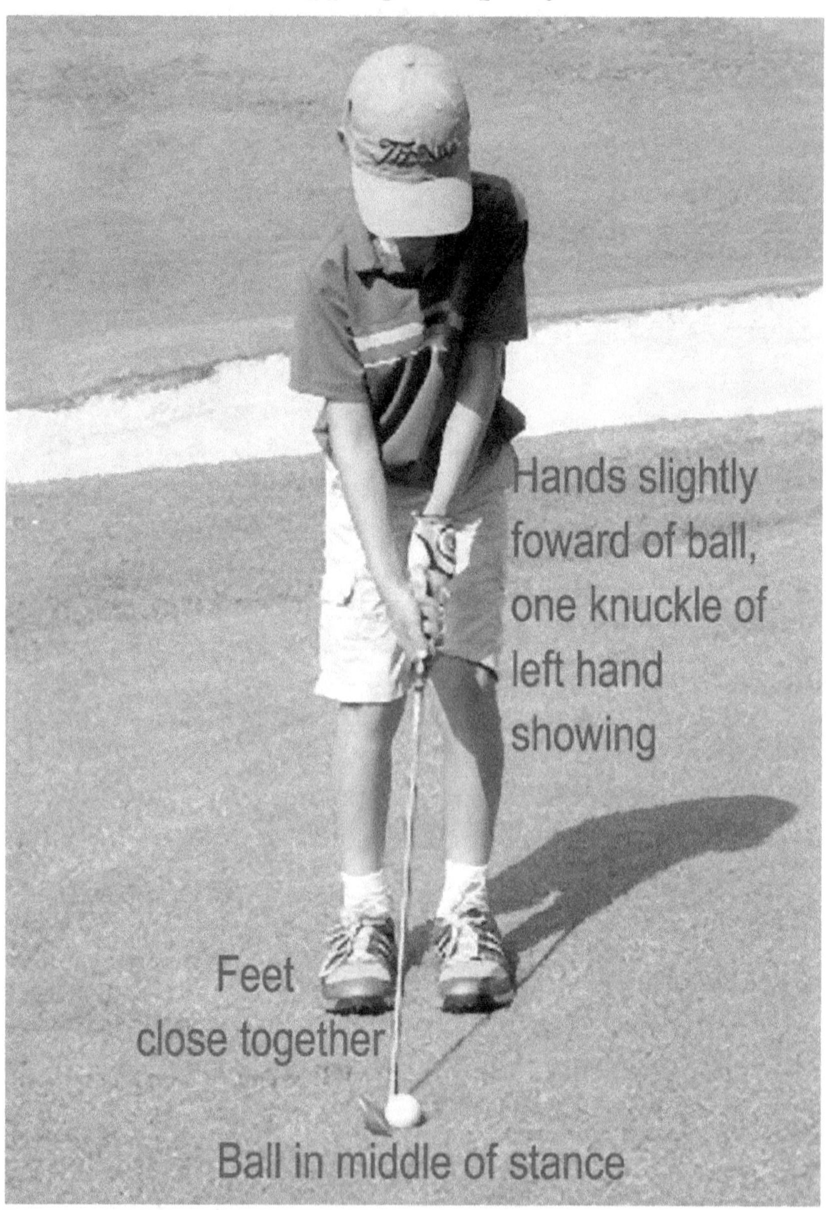

Chip when you are very close to the green to carry the ball in the air onto the green where it can then roll toward the hole. Clubs used: 7, 8, 9, pw and sw.

Pitching

Pitching the golf ball is hitting the ball a short distance and with a high trajectory much like an underhanded toss so the ball flies high and then lands softly on the green.

You will always use a wedge for these shots. The wedge has a lot of loft and hits the ball high into the air for a short distance and then lands it softly so it doesn't roll much on the green. You will need to hit the ball high and land it softly whenever you are close to the green and in the "rough" (long grass).

The wedges allow you to make a pretty big swing without hitting the ball very far. This is important when you are in the rough next to the green. You need to be able to swing hard to get through the long grass, but also hit the ball high and soft. This can only be done with the high lofted clubs known as wedges.

The sand wedge

The sand wedge is the wedge provided in most junior sets. It is good to use whenever your ball is sitting down in the tall grass or rough around the green.

A sand wedge can be swung with more speed, which gets through the resistance of the grass and it will pop the ball high up in the air and also land it softly on the green.

Pitching technique

You can use the chipping technique of just using arms and shoulders when you are very close to the green with the sand wedge, but when you are further from the hole there will be a longer yardage where that technique no longer works. You won't be able to hit the ball far enough with just arms and shoulders.

You will need to create some "hinge" with your wrists and elbow. This is the same as creating an 'L' in the backswing. You let your wrists hinge and right arm fold to create some extra power, which is needed to go longer distances. Create an 'L' halfway back to let the club head swing a further distance so you can get more controlled speed into the ball.

On the follow through, try to keep the clubface pointing at the sky well into your follow through in order to keep loft on the club and keep the ball going up high in the air.

Wedge selection

Once you become an experienced golfer and start to use a full set of 14 clubs you will be able to use a selection of 4 different clubs for pitching. Typically, the wedges will have the following lofts. Loft is the angle between the clubface and the shaft.

The more loft a club has the higher and less far it will hit the ball when you make a full swing.

- Pitching wedge = 47 degrees loft
- Gap Wedge = 50 degrees loft
- Sand Wedge = 56 degrees loft
- Lob Wedge = 60 degrees loft

You will mostly use the sand wedge to pitch when you are further away from the edge of the green and need to carry the ball a longer distance in the air to get on the green.

When you are very close to a green and have a good lie on short grass, chip using your seven iron or another lower lofted club. The ball will go a short distance in the air and roll a longer distance on the green.

Side hill, Uphill, Downhill lies.

A big challenge to chipping and pitching is constantly playing from different uphill, downhill and sidehill lies. Around every green there are a variety of different slopes where your ball can stop. Playing off a slope will affect the trajectory of your shot differently than playing from a flat lie.

Basically hitting from an upslope will make your ball fly higher and a shorter distance than if you were playing off flat ground with the same swing and club.

Pitching from an upslope with a nine iron will actually make the ball react more like a sand wedge because you have to add the angle of the upslope to the angle of the clubface.

NOTE: In the pictures showing two balls the white balls show the 'normal' ball flight and the yellow balls show the way the slope tends to influence the ball flight.

Hitting from a downslope will make your ball fly lower in relation to a flat lie.

Pitching from a downslope will be the opposite of an upslope and make a sand wedge fly lower and more like a nine iron. The loft on the club at impact with the ball is less when you swing along the down slope.

Hitting from a side hill slope with the ball above your feet will make the ball fly more to the left. Hitting from a side hill slope with the ball below your feet will make the ball fly slightly to the right

Pitching drill

To get a good understanding and visual feel for varying and controlling your distances with the wedge clubs try this great pitching drill at the driving range.

You will need a few towels, some golf balls and your wedge club(s). Place a towel every 10 yards out to a distance of 70 yards.

Using a sand wedge, hit 10 shots to each towel starting from the closest at 10-yards distance and gradually hit out to the 70-yard towel.

You may even need to use a pitching wedge to go to the 60 or 70-yard distances.

Once you hit 10 balls to each towel try to hit one ball to each towel starting with the 10-yard or 70-yard towel.

Next try to hit to each towel in a random order. Do this drill often in practice sessions to achieve good distance control for short shots with your wedges.

Tip for good distance control

Match the length of your back swing to the length of your follow through for whichever distance you are hitting to.

For a short pitch, if you swing your club head three feet back from the ball then make sure you swing the club head three feet past the ball when you follow though.

For a medium pitch, if you swing halfway back to the "L" position, then finish your swing to the halfway though "L" position.

For a long pitch, if you make a full back swing you then need to finish into a full follow through position.

Pitch shot set up

Use this shot to loft the ball high in the air and land it softly on the green. A great shot to use from bad lies such as in deep rough around the greens. Clubs used: All wedges including pw, gw, sw and lob wedge.

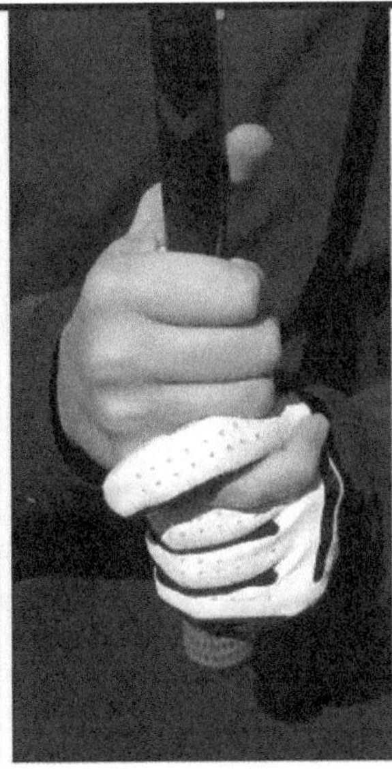

Lesson 4
SAND SHOTS

Lesson 4 - SAND SHOTS

What you will need.

- Sand wedge
- A five, six or seven iron.
- A few golf balls.
- A place to practice. a golf course practice area.

Greenside bunker shots

The bunkers located right next to the green are called greenside bunkers. (See page 242) Greenside bunkers require a special technique to get the ball out successfully.

Our goal is to loft the ball high in the air and then land it softly on the green so it hopefully gets close to the hole without rolling too much or going over the green.

We use a sand wedge for this shot. It has lots of loft. The clubface points high up to the sky. This club creates a shot that would resemble more of an underhanded toss with a ball rather than a fastball pitch of a ball. The underhanded toss would have a lot better chance of getting close to the hole, right?

The big difference between this shot technique and other golf shots is that the club head contacts the sand before the ball. Doing this helps to make the ball fly slowly in the air.

Sand 'explosion' shot

We try to slide the club head into the sand before striking the ball.

The club head will enter the sand at the line behind the ball and come up well beyond the line at the ball.

When you practice DO NOT use sticks. Draw lines in the sand.

The sand and the club head work together to lift the ball out like a soft underhanded toss of the ball. The sand on the clubface through impact helps take some speed off the ball so it travels slowly in the air.

The basics of good technique

Hands

First we are going to set up with our hands exactly over the club head and not in front of or behind the club head. This will expose the bounce (bottom) of the sand wedge and help it slide and skim through the sand without digging down into the sand.

We then turn our body slightly toward the target.

The rules for a hazard say you cannot ground your club in the hazard before playing your shot. You must hold the club head a little above the sand while standing over your shot.

Feet

Next, let's wiggle our feet into the sand. This helps us sense the firmness of the sand and also keeps our legs and feet steady and still.

Wiggling your feet into the sand will help keep your legs still during your swing, which is important in getting the club head to enter the sand at the exact right moment before getting to the ball.

Some sand is heavy when wet after rainstorms or it can also be light and fluffy when dry and powdery on a sunny day. Digging in with your feet will help you sense the force needed to get the club through the sand.

You will learn what I mean with lots of practice.

Swing

Use a long back swing and follow through for sand shots. Make a full swing with your hands over your right shoulder in the back swing and a full follow through with your hands over your left shoulder at the finish.

The sand will slow your club head once it starts into the sand so it is important to try and keep the club head moving through the sand using a long back swing and long follow through.

Many beginning juniors make a good long back swing, but then stop their club in the sand when they are at the ball. The club head loses speed and the ball stays in the bunker or goes less than the desired distance to the hole.

Finish your swing

The biggest mistake with learning bunker shots is slowing down or stopping with the club head at the ball. You must swing through the sand without stopping at the ball into a nice full finish position.

Clubface points up

The last big key to greenside bunker shots is to keep the clubface pointing to the sky while swinging through the ball. This keeps plenty of loft on the club in order to lift the ball up and out of deep bunkers.

Bunkers are hazards, which means they are intended to penalize your score for entering them, but with proper technique you can avoid making a high score.

Greenside bunker shot set up keys

Used from a greenside bunker this shot lofts the ball in the air and only goes a short distance. Club used: sand wedge

Fairway bunkers

The golf course will have fairway bunkers located in and along the fairways. We will call bunkers that are further than 20-30 yards from the green 'fairway bunkers'. The hole layout on page 242 shows the location of these bunkers.

You usually want to hit the ball a longer distance from a fairway bunker than from a greenside bunker so we use a different technique.

When hitting out of a fairway bunker we use the same technique as hitting an iron or fairway wood shot where the club head must hit the ball first and then the ground.

You may not ground your club in a fairway bunker, but you can and should wiggle your feet into the sand just like a greenside bunker shot. This will stabilize your feet and legs and help you make good contact with the ball.

So remember, there are two kinds of bunker shots.

- Short, soft greenside bunker shots where you hit the sand behind the ball first and,
- Longer fairway bunker shots where you hit the ball first.

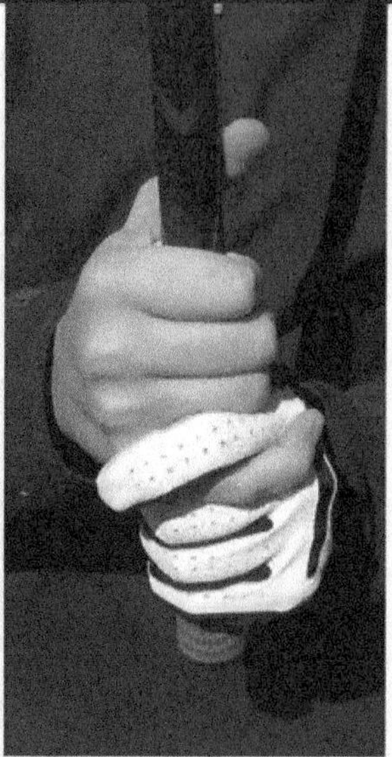

Lesson 5
FULL SWING

Lesson 5 - FULL SWING

What you will need.

- A five iron
- A driver
- Some golf balls
- Some tees
- Golf shoes or sneakers
- A place to hit shots safely - a golf course practice area. A driving range

Every golfer enjoys hitting a good solidly struck shot that flies toward the target. This can be done with a driver, fairway wood, hybrid or any of the irons.

Hitting the ball solid and straight is a great feeling and what we always try to do each time we play a shot.

To hit the ball consistently well each time we must first concentrate on achieving the correct set up position for the shot we are trying to play.

The set up

The set up is how we stand to the ball before we even begin to start swinging and it is the most important fundamental to learning and playing golf.

The setup includes these 4 fundamentals:

1. Grip
2. Posture
3. Alignment
4. Ball Position

You will learn to play different shots and sometimes they require slightly different set ups.

So remember from our previous lessons, set up is not always the same for all shots, but is still the most important fundamental for all of the different shots you will play.

Address position

The set up is also known as the 'address position' and is how you stand to the ball before you even start to swing. It includes getting the proper posture, grip, alignment, and ball position for each shot.

Setting up correctly allows you to swing the club properly for whichever shot you are trying to make, whether it is a long drive or a short putt. So remember; set up, set up, set up.

You should concentrate most of your early learning on correct set up positions for each of the six different shots.

Okay, so let's get started learning the four fundamentals of a good set up.

Interlock Grip

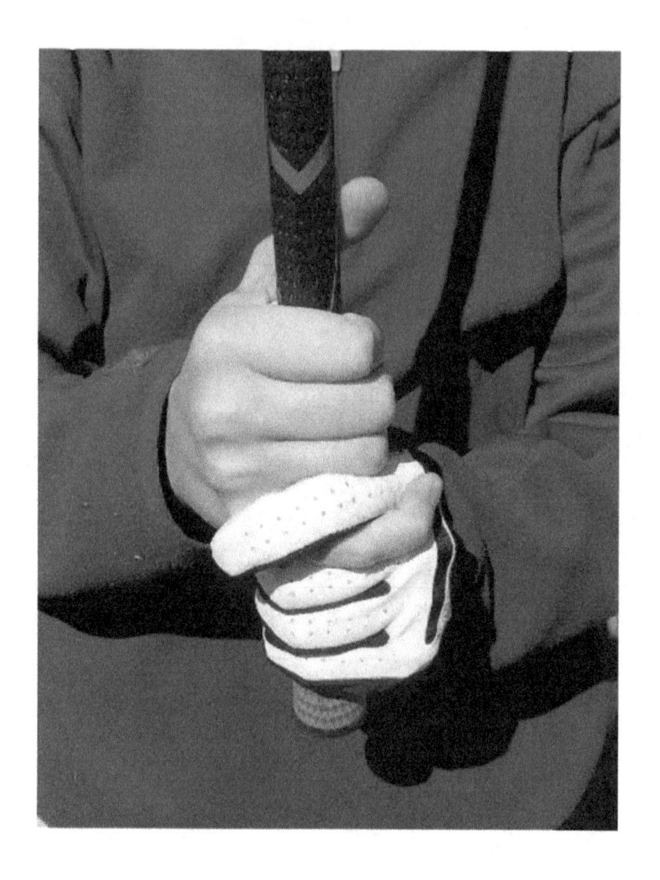

Right hand

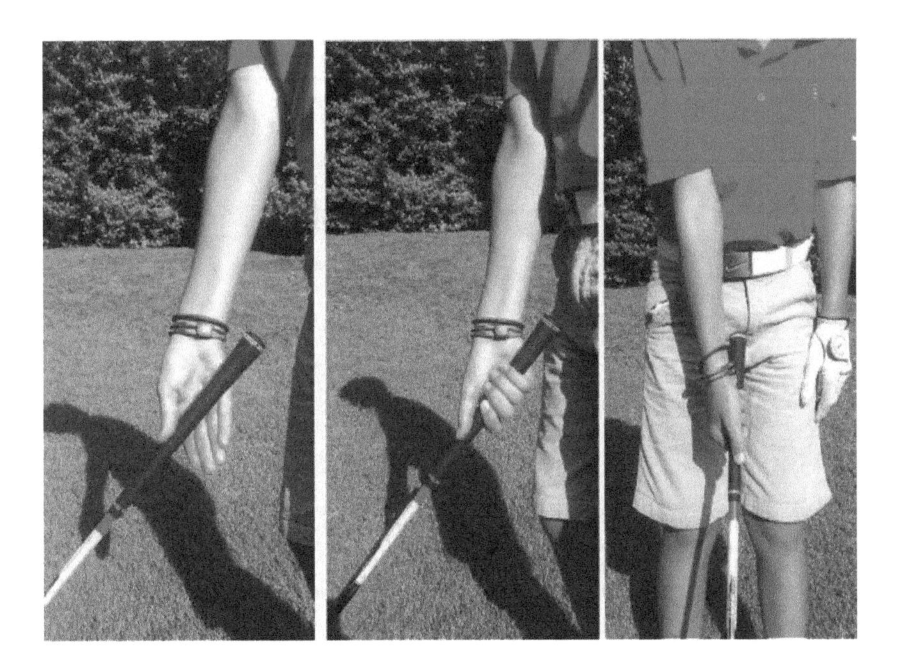

Your right hand grips the club where your fingers meet the palm of your hand. Check out the position of the thumb, on top and a little to the left side.

Left hand

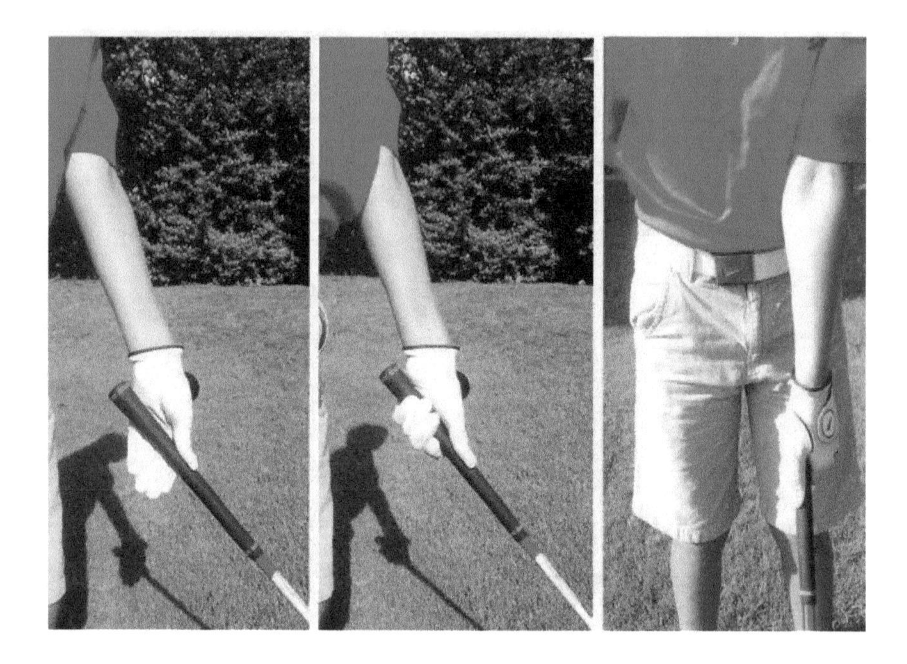

Your left hand grips the club where the fingers meet the palm of your hand. See where the thumb is: on top and a little to the right side.

Both hands

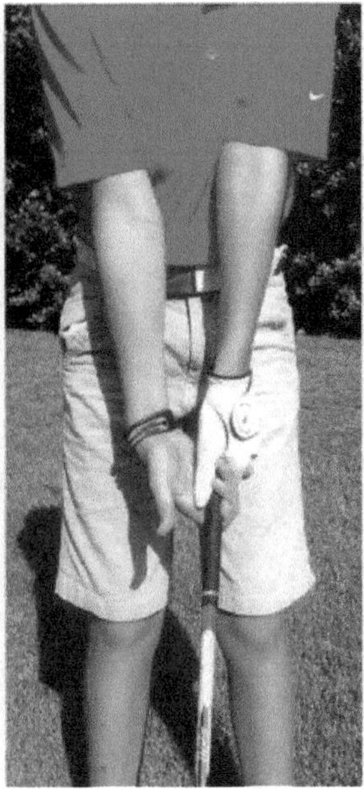
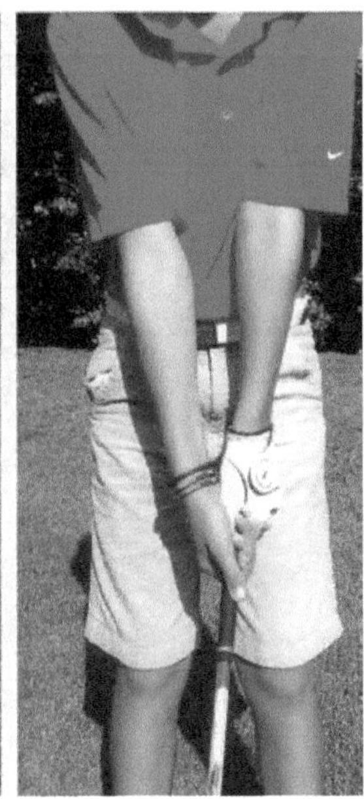

Now grip the club with both hands like this. 'Interlock' the pinky finger of your right hand with the index finger of your left hand as shown page 108.

When you place the club head on the ground and the clubface is aligned directly at the target you should be able to see two or three knuckles of your left hand when you look down.

Posture

Posture is how we position our body, arms and stance (feet) while standing at the ball. Our goal with good posture is to be balanced and able to swing athletically without losing our balance.

If we are falling over during our swing because we don't have good balance then we won't hit the ball in the center of the clubface while swinging with good athletic speed. Especially for those long drives you will want to hit.

Achieving good posture takes practice.

This is NOT good. His arms are too close to his body and he's standing too straight.

Too straight and leaning backwards will cause him to be off balance and fall backwards while he swings.

This is NOT good. He's bent over too much.

Too much bend at the hips has too much weight leaning forward and will cause him to be off balance and fall forward when he swings the club.

This is NOT good. His hands are to close too his body.

With your arms too close to your body you will not be able to swing your arms freely and athletically to create speed in the club head.

This is NOT good either. He's reaching out too far.

Reaching too far will tend to put too much weight on your toes and you will fall forward during your swing and not consistently hit the ball in the middle of the clubface.

So, as you can see, there are many ways to do it wrong!

Now let's see how to achieve good, balanced posture.

How to achieve good posture

Look at Nick in a "basketball" defensive posture.

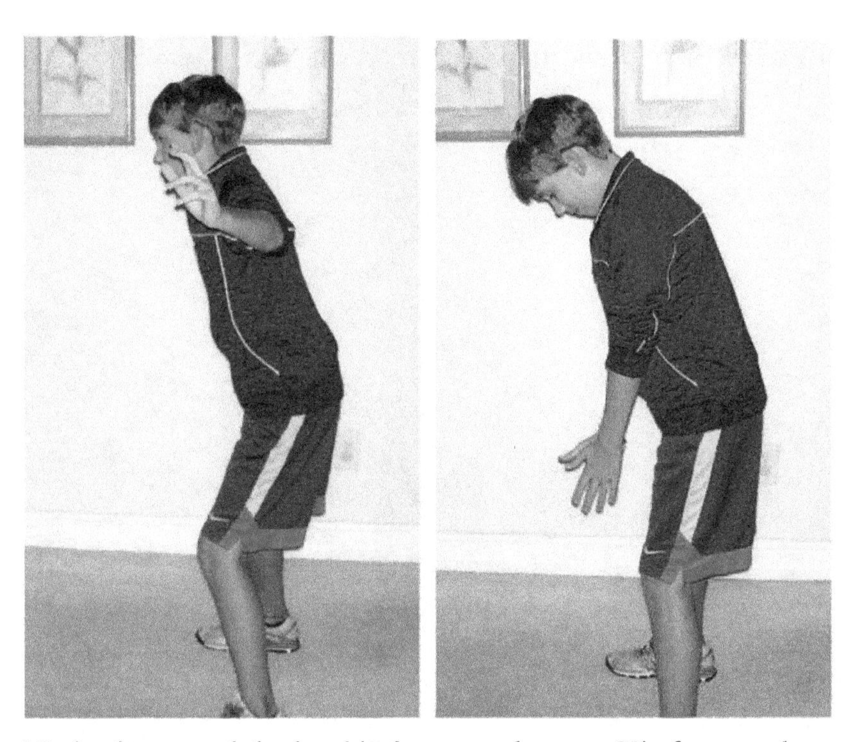

Notice how much he has his feet spread apart. His feet are about shoulder width apart. He has a little bend in his knees and some bend at the hips.

Overall, his weight is centered and balanced. This means he does not have his weight too much leaning forward toward his toes or too much falling back on his heels.

He's also not leaning to the left or to the right.

So he is balanced and ready to move in any direction and it would be hard to push him over because he is balanced so nicely.

Good posture makes it possible to keep your balance when you swing.

So practice this balanced 'playing basketball defense' posture with a slight bend in the knees and hips and with your feet shoulder width apart.

Next, and the final part of good posture, is to let your arms hang down from your shoulders.

Here's what good posture looks like when you are setting up to the ball with a driver.

Alignment

Alignment is properly aiming the clubface and your body toward the target.

In golf, beginners and professionals are always working hard to get their alignment correct for each shot.

Clubface alignment

Clubface alignment is also important to make the ball go towards your target.

Here are some common examples of bad clubface alignment.

This is a "closed" clubface. It is aimed to the left of the target line and the ball will go left.

The target line is an imaginary line from your target.

This is an "open" clubface. It is aimed to the right of the target and the ball will go to the right.

Club shaft alignment

In aligning the clubface you must also position the shaft correctly.

Here the shaft is leaning too far forward.

This is leaning too far back.

Setting the shaft too far forward or back places your hands in the wrong position at address.

Correct clubface and shaft alignment

The front edge on the bottom of the clubface is at a 90-degree angle in relation to the target line.

The shaft is pretty close to straight, but just slightly leaning forward.

Shoulders and arms

The next big fundamental to concentrate on is to make sure your forearms are level at address. This means that when you look in a mirror you can barely see your left arm when looking from behind down the target line

Notice how you can see only Nick's back arm. This will make a lot of good things happen when you swing the club so try to copy the picture of Nick in a mirror for a good set up.

Also notice that Nick's feet and shoulders are all parallel to the target line as shown by the blue stick across his shoulders and along his feet. The blue stick in front of the ball represents the target line.

Ball position

The next important step to set up is ball position. This means where the ball lies in between your feet while you stand to the ball.

Ball position for irons

Stand with your feet together and a ball in the middle of your feet. Place the club behind the ball.

Then take a small step to the left with your left foot and a small step to the right with your right foot. Now the club is exactly in the middle of your feet. This is a great way to begin for hitting irons.

Ball position for woods

For the woods and driver start with your feet together and then take a small step to the left with your left foot but take a slightly bigger step to the right with your right foot.

Now see the picture, your ball and club head are slightly closer to the left foot than the right foot when viewed from face on. This is how to learn playing your woods and driver.

Some things to remember

The best professional golfers play their shots the same way as you are learning in this chapter. They concentrate on a good set up which means good posture, grip, alignment, and ball position.

When you learn to set up properly for each shot you will be able to swing athletically and hit a good solid shots.

To hit good solid shots the ball must be struck in the center of the clubface, also called the sweet spot.

The clubface must be closely aligned to the target when it strikes the ball.

You must swing the club with the correct amount of speed to produce the correct distance for the shot you chose to play.

You will achieve much success with your shots by simply setting up correctly before you hit each shot

Balance

Balance in golf means being able to swing with some speed while also moving your weight toward the target without falling over or moving your feet from their starting position.

Just like when you walk on a balance beam or try to walk along a street curb you have to keep your weight from moving too much to the sides so you don't fall over.

While swinging a golf club you must first swing the club back while keeping your weight centered and then swing down and through the ball while turning your chest and belt buckle toward the target as well as feeling all your weight move over to your left foot.

A good practice drill is to practice throwing a ball to your left (for right handed player). I'll cover this in more detail in the 'Practice Drills', but here's a quick look.

Balanced start

To begin, get into an athletic posture with a little bend in the knees and a little bend at the hips. Next, simply hold the ball out in front of you then swing your arm back and through releasing the ball much like you were skipping a stone or throwing a baseball using a sidearm throwing motion.

Balanced finish

Look in the SWING PRACTICE DRILLS chapter to learn more about how this drill is performed.

Full swing - Irons

Iron shot fundamentals

When using an iron you want the clubface to hit the ball first then the ground.

Each iron is designed to hit the ball a different height and distance.

When the ball bounces off the face of the club the loft of the club will determine how high and how far the ball flies.

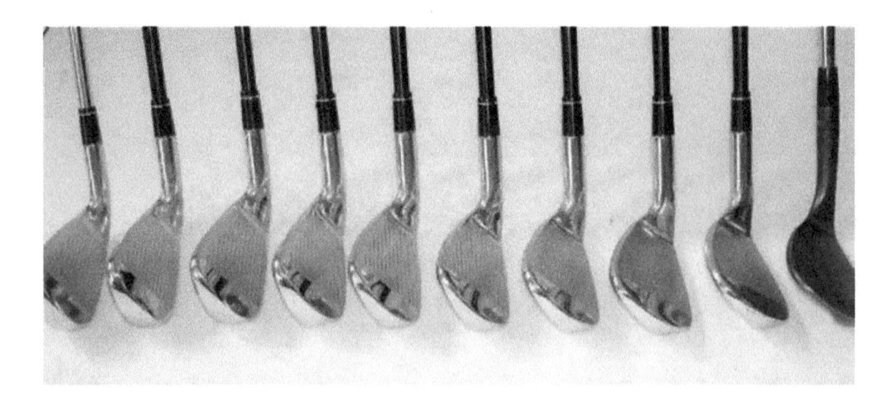

The more loft, the higher the ball flight. The longer irons (on the left in this picture) will hit the ball lower and further than the shorter irons on the right.

A full set of irons is designed so that there is about a ten-yard difference in ball flight distance from one to the next.

Know your distance

A major part of good iron strategy into any green is to know the distance you will need to hit your shot and then to pick the right club.

Look for yardage markers

As you walk down each fairway be aware of the yardage markings on the ground. These can be located on sprinkler heads or specific yardage markers on each fairway and on each par 3 teeing ground.

Usually every course will have a yardage marker for the 100, 150, and 200-yard distances for each hole. These markers are usually measured to the middle of each green for every hole. Most courses have these markers in the middle of the fairway as shown on page 242.

As you walk down the fairway to your ball find the nearest yardage marker to your ball. Take long strides (steps) to count the number of yards from the marker to your ball. Add or subtract the number of strides to get a good yardage figure.

Three other things to consider besides yardage

Once you have the actual yardage you will then need to factor in other conditions such as the **lie of the ball, wind, and slopes.** Judging how the lie of the ball affects the shot distance is the most difficult and is especially tricky when in the rough.

Ball in the rough

Generally, when the ball is sitting **down low in heavy rough** it will force you to take one or two extra clubs (maybe a 7 iron instead of a 9 iron). You may also have to rely on the ball rolling or running up to the green instead of flying all the way to the hole. Usually the ball will come out on a lower flight and have no backspin so it will want to roll more than a shot hit from the fairway.

However, when a ball is sitting high **on top of the grass in the rough** it will lead to what we call a **'flier'** lie. The ball will fly further in the air and also have less spin when it lands. In this case, you will need to take one or two less club (maybe hit a 9 iron instead of a 7 iron).

How conditions in the rough will affect the ball's flight and distance in each of these situations is difficult to determine. You will need some golf experience to learn these shots.

Wind

Let's say the yardage you want to play calls for a 9-iron. Usually, when the wind is gentle at 5 to 10 mph you will need to either add a club (hit an 8-iron instead of 9) if your shot is into the wind, or, subtract a club (hit a 9-iron instead of 8) if your shot is down wind.

When the winds are stronger you may need to factor more than just one extra club difference for the wind.

Uphill or downhill

If you have an uphill shot you have to add one or two clubs (maybe hit a 7-iron instead of a 9) to your distance. If you are going down hill subtract one or two clubs (maybe hit a wedge instead of a 9) from your distance.

Correct club selection is a challenge

In review, the main factors you will need to decide are yardage, lie of the ball, wind, and slopes. The real art and science of playing great golf and what makes it so challenging is that all of these factors must be applied to each shot throughout your round.

It sounds like a lot of thinking doesn't it? But with experience you can process all of these factors in just a few seconds and play your shots without much delay.

Swing positions

Let's use a 5 iron to begin learning how to swing the club.

Always, before swinging, start by establishing your set up position with good posture, a good grip, and good alignment.

Place the club head exactly in the middle of your stance.

To learn the basic swinging motion you can also practice without having a ball on the ground.

Position A

Next you need to learn to swing your club to these positions. First, start at set up. Then swing to position A.

This is where you want the club to move through as you make a full swinging motion. See the club on Nick's stance line? Make your club shaft match the direction of that club at position A.

His left arm is extended straight and his right arm is slightly folded and also his club shaft is tilted and pointing at the target line.

At the top

Next finish swinging to the top by feeling your hands over your right shoulder with your left arm still extended and right arm folded. His shoulders have turned until his left shoulder is under his chin.

Position B

Then go to position B as shown in the picture.

Notice how nick has made a backward "L" with his right arm and the club.

Finish the swing

You can let your head and body rotate toward the target as you swing past the ground where the ball would normally be. Finish with your body and head facing the target.

All of your weight should move onto your left leg as you swing through. You can come up on your right toe as you finish, but keep it in place.

Make several practice swings this way back and through making a full motion back and through. Your weight should move onto your left foot as you swing through and turn to the finish.

Next do this without your head or feet moving while you make this back swing motion. Not moving your head or feet on the back swing will help you learn to swing in balance and consistently hit the ball solid. Moving your feet usually means you are trying to keep yourself from falling over and therefore swinging out of balance.

Full swing with irons set up keys

Use your irons whenever hitting off the ground or a tee to a specific distance.

Full swing - Driver

Hitting the golf ball really far is one of the most fun aspects of golf and especially for a junior golfer. No other sport boasts being able to hit a ball so far. The longest hitting drivers of the ball can now hit a golf ball over 450 yards.

You will get really excited when you are able to hit the golf ball farther than you ever did with a baseball or tennis ball. So let's get started and learn the most important fundamentals of learning to hit the driver.

You tee the ball up so the driver will swing through the ball without ever touching the ground.

The newer deep face drivers are designed so that the sweet spot is near the middle of the clubface. This is where you want the driver to meet the ball.

Driver set up

DRIVER

5 IRON

The set up is similar to your iron set up except now you widen your stance by moving your right foot more to the right by about 4-5 inches.

The ball position now looks like it is more forward or closer to your left foot in your stance when you look at it face on in the mirror.

This wider stance will help you make an athletic swing with speed and power while also keeping your balance so you can hit the ball long and solid.

Driver set up keys

When to use: Off the tee for par 4's, 5's and some par 3's.

How to tee up the ball

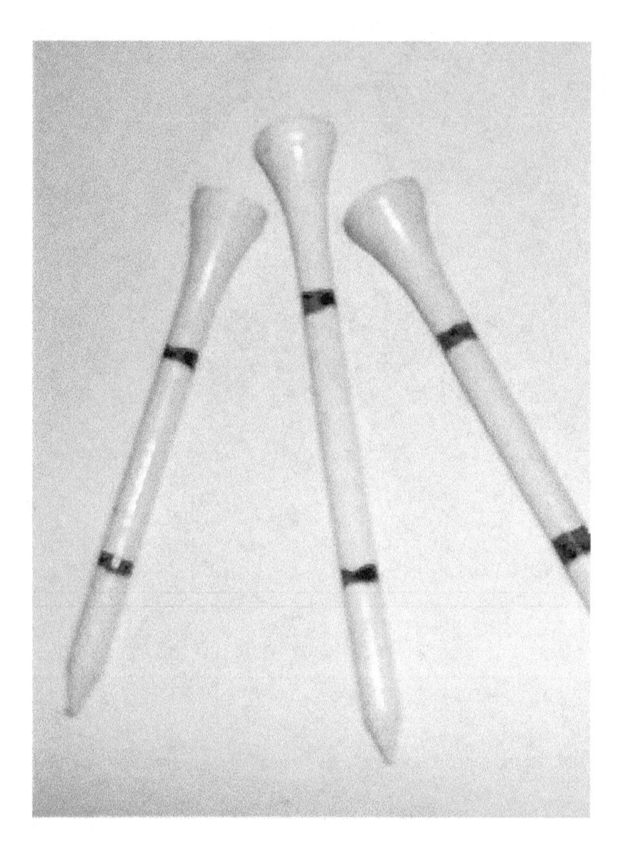

A good trick for teeing the same every time is to use a sharpie marker and draw a line around some of your golf tees about 2 and one half inches down from the top of the tee. When you tee the ball only put the tee in the ground as far as the line.

You can do the same for your irons when you tee off on a short hole. Draw the line about one half inch from the top for irons.

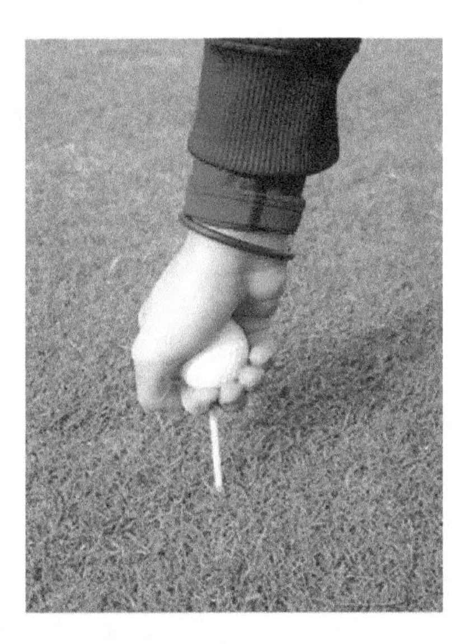

Notice how to we hold the ball and tee together before we begin teeing our ball.

Hold the ball and tee together in the palm of your hand and then push straight down on the ball to put the tee in the ground.

Holding the ball against the tee while you push the tee into the ground is the easiest and fastest way to get the tee into the ground with the ball on top of it each time.

Driver swing keys

Swing with speed

The first step for good long hitting drives is to swing the golf club with some good speed. Once you get into your driver set up, practice making some swings without a ball and see if you can create a swoosh sound with the club head when it is approaching the ball area.

The big key to getting a good swoosh sound is to make a full backswing and then go to a full follow through. You must make a full motion in order to gain speed into the ball.

Swing your club all the way back so that your hands swing back over your right shoulder and your left shoulder is in under your chin in the back swing.

Finish balanced

When you swing down and through, finish with your hands over your left shoulder, your right shoulder under your chin and your chest facing in the direction of the target area you are hitting to.

Finish facing the target without losing your balance or moving your feet and with your weight over your front leg

The last big key to good solid contact when making a full driver swing with lots of speed is to try to keep your head steady and in the same place as you make a full motion back and through.

Keep your head still and steady on the back swing and then let your head rotate with the follow through after striking the ball so that your head and body face the target at the finish of your follow through.

Practice making a full back and thru motion while keeping your head steady.

Review

Remember these driver fundamentals.

- Move your right foot wider so your stance is wider than with your irons.
- Make a full backswing and follow through.
- Make a swoosh sound with the club head at ball to ensure speed.
- Swing through to a balanced full finish position.
- Tee the ball half way over the top line of club.
- Keep your head still while making a full swing.

Swing practice drills

Always practice with a purpose and have some fundamentals to work on in order to get better.

Here is a list of great practice drills to work on while swinging the club. These drills all focus on key fundamentals of a good golf swing and every great golfer thinks about these swing keys from time to time to help improve their swing and ball striking skills.

You can do these drills while hitting balls at the practice range and you can also do them in your back yard without even hitting a ball.

Write these tips in a practice notebook and store it your golf bag. Review each of them when you go to practice.

An important part of practice is to always have some key fundamentals to work on and never go to practice without having a good idea of what you are supposed to do in order to get better.

Go through this list when you practice and do at least 15 swings for each different tip.

Use your shadow

You can use your shadow to learn and maintain a steady head while swinging your club.

Turn your back to the sun so you have your shadow in front of you. Put a golf ball on the shadow of your head.

Next, begin swinging the club back and forth keeping the shadow of your head on the ball.

A nice steady head will help you repeat a consistent impact on the ball.

Reach back with the club

Swing 15 times getting club to parallel and toe up position.

The tilted 'L;

Swing 15 times creating a tilted "L" half way into the back swing and . . .

.... a tilted backward "L" halfway through in the through swing.

Maintain an extended left arm during back swing and extended right arm in through swing.

Turn your shoulders

Now swing 15 times swinging into a full back swing with a full shoulder turn and with your hands over your right shoulder, then down and through into a full follow through position with a full shoulder turn and hands your over left shoulder

A balanced finish

Swing 15 times back and through holding a balanced finish position with your weight on left leg and facing target and without moving the position of your feet except to come up on your back foot to your toe.

Brush the grass

Practice swinging and concentrate on brushing the grass all the way down to where the blades of grass meet the ground. You want to be able to brush the grass down where it grows from the ground and not just the top of the grass blades.

Try to brush the grass with the club head as you swing down past the grass where the ball would normally be.

We don't want to just hit the top of the grass or our club won't hit the ball on the sweet spot. The club head needs to be closer to the ground to lift the ball.

We want to be able to swing the club head like an airplane coming in for a landing and then taking off again

We are trying to make a full motion with our arms back and through by swinging our hands all the way over each shoulder.

We are trying to brush the grass with the club head, trying to maintain balance by not moving our feet from where they started, and trying to turn our body towards the target as we follow through into a full balanced finish position. Sounds like a lot but it's really simple once you do it correctly a few times.

Once you can make the basic swinging motion of brushing the grass and not moving your head or feet while also keeping your balance, try to add more speed. See how fast you can swing and brush the grass while also keeping your balance.

Keep a good grip

Swing 15 times maintaining a good grip without your hands slipping or coming off the grip

Create club head speed.

Swing 15 times trying to create some speed in the club head with your driver while also moving into your nice balanced finish position. Listen for the "swish" where the club would be hitting the ball. The louder the swish, the faster the club head speed, the longer the drive!

Balance

Swinging in balance means being able to make a swing without tipping or leaning over.

As you swing and turn, your weight should move over to your left foot as you fully unwind and face your body toward your target.

You must also maintain a good athletic posture when you swing.

Your weight shouldn't move to your toes, or back on your heels, or stay on your right foot.

Two big set up keys to swinging in balance are proper posture and stance width when you address the ball. Remember to set up like a basketball player playing defense. Your feet shoulder width apart. Your weight centered in the middle of your feet and not toward your toes or toward your heels. Your weight spread equally between your left and right feet.

If you swing in balance then you will more consistently hit the ball in the middle of the clubface and hit a lot of great golf shots.

Swinging out of balance means we are moving incorrectly and results in bad golf shots.

Practice drill for balance

So let's get started to get the feel of good balance by showing you how to unwind your body toward the target, move your weight to your left foot, and hold a balanced finish position.

Here is a simple drill to learn how to 1. Use your feet, 2. Unwind your body, and 3. Move your weight toward the target.

Note to lefties: simply switch hands and throw left to right.

You can practice this drill in the back yard for hours each week without ever hitting a golf ball to learn the sensation of swinging in balance. Then you will soon see it carry over to your golf shots as they improve at the course.

Study the pictures in this sequence of Nick throwing a ball. With this drill we want to learn to swing a golf club with a motion similar to throwing a ball while turning our body and without losing our balance while keeping our feet in place.

Start

To begin, get into an athletic posture with a little bend in the knees and a little bend at the hips and hold the ball out in front of you. Now swing your arm back.

Swing back & throw

Throw the ball as if you were pitching sidearm to a baseball catcher just to your left.

Once you release the ball, finish off the motion with a full turn of your body to the left.

Also, with the turn of your body you can let your right heel come off the ground so you are balanced and with all of you weight in the middle of the outside of your left foot.

This is the most efficient way to athletically throw with both power and accuracy. Next we want to transfer this feeling while swinging our golf club.

If while throwing or swinging you tip forward on your toes or back on your heels you will probably have to take a step to catch yourself from falling over. Check to make sure you have maintained your good athletic posture without too much or too little bend in your knees or hips.

Keep repeating this drill until you can master it and then try to transfer this feeling while you swing one of your golf clubs.

You can practice throwing whiffle balls or swinging a club without hitting any balls in your backyard to get better at this drill for good athletic power with balance.

Practice impact

A good drill is to practice impact. You can do this in front of a mirror to help you see yourself or have someone take your picture

Impact is how you look while your club is striking the ball and looks similar to the address position.

Here is the address position.

Here is the correct position at impact.

Some key things to look for are:

1. Your clubface is square to the target line.

2. Your left arm and club shaft form a vertical straight line up from the ball.

3. Your head is behind the ball.

4. Your hips have slightly turned toward the target.

Getting the first key is important because you learn clubface awareness and how to square up the clubface at the ball.

Getting the second key right teaches you how to release the shaft at the right time and goes hand in hand with helping to learn to square the clubface for both distance and accuracy.

PLAYING THE GAME

PLAYING THE GAME

The golf course

The golf course facility is made up of many different areas which you need to become familiar with and learn how to use. These areas include:

- The golf course
- Driving range
- Putting green
- Clubhouse
- Cart barn
- Maintenance facility
- Parking lot

The clubhouse

The clubhouse usually includes a pro shop where you check in, a restaurant, locker rooms, and restrooms.

The Pro shop

The Pro Shop is where you begin once you arrive. It is here you will need to check in before your tee time and pay a fee to play the course or pay to use the driving range.

Locker room and rest rooms

Not all golf courses have locker rooms where you can store things in a locker, but almost all have rest rooms. It is always best to use the rest room before going on the course as you will be on the course for a long time and there are few, if any, restrooms located on the course.

The driving range

The driving range is the practice and warm up area where you can either practice for an extended time or just go to warm up before you play the course. Warming up means hitting about 40-60 balls.

This helps your muscles stretch and warm up which will help you make solid contact and establish good timing to hit the ball solid with each swing.

A good warm up on the driving range followed by some chipping and putting on the practice green takes about 30 minutes.

The driving range is also a practice facility when you just want to practice for an extended time without going on the course. For a good practice session you will want to hit 100-120 balls followed by some chipping and putting.

A good practice session of 100-120 balls on the range followed by chipping and putting practice will take one or two hours. It is always good to practice improving your skills in a practice session as well as playing the course.

As a junior you can usually practice much more than playing

because you can always practice at your home with chipping, putting and swinging in the backyard. So practice, practice, practice when and wherever you can!!!

The practice putting green

A green located near the clubhouse is a warm up and practice area especially for chipping and putting. Practicing some putting before you play will help you adjust to the speed of the golf course greens and learn how to judge the break for the type of grass and amount of slopes on the greens you will be playing that day.

Because all courses are different, this is important to helping you make some two putts and maybe even some one putts on the course. Remember, taking three or more putts on any green is bad for your score.

Also, hitting a few chips will show you how firm the greens are when the ball bounces and how much the ball will roll out based on the slopes and the speed of the greens.

The cart barn and equipment sheds

The cart barn is where all the golf carts are stored. Most of us think of a barn as a place for horses, cows, or chickens, but at a golf course it is basically a big garage area where the golf carts are stored. Also, it doesn't look like a barn either, but might only look like a big garage.

An 18 hole golf course will usually have 75 golf carts because that is the maximum number of carts that can be on the course at one time when lots of people are playing on a nice, busy, sunny day.

It is important for juniors to know that golf carts can be dangerous and not to ever touch the pedals on a golf cart.

You should only be in a golf cart when an adult is already in the cart.

On the golf course, you should never be in the golf cart by yourself or without an adult as it can suddenly start rolling on a slope or you can accidentally hit the pedals and the cart will start moving.

Never stand in front or behind a golf cart because it may start rolling. Be extremely careful near golf carts, as they can be very dangerous!

What to wear on the course

You always want to dress correctly for the type of weather you will be playing in. If it is hot light colored shirts and shorts are always good. Hot weather clothing includes:

- Hat
- Sunglasses
- Sunscreen
- Collared golf shirt
- Golf shoes or sneakers
- Non-blue jeans or shorts

When it is cold wear "layers" of clothing instead of just one big jacket.

- A thermal shirt & bottoms
- Long sleeve turtleneck shirt
- A sweater
- Windbreaker
- Warm socks
- Winter golf gloves
- Knit cap
- Earmuffs

This way you can always adjust when the temperature changes.

Many courses do not allow blue jeans or t-shirts so a collared golf shirt and non-blue jean pants, shorts or skirts should be worn at nice courses.

You also need good foot support so wear sneakers or golf shoes if you have them. Never wear flip flops, boots, soccer or baseball cleats to play golf.

What to Carry in your golf bag

Your golf bag has lots of pockets. You should always check that you have all the items you will need before you leave your home. It is especially important to carry a water bottle, sunscreen and a hat during the hot summer.

Pack a snack or two to help maintain your concentration and energy level while on the course. Golf takes about 4 hours to play and you will get tired without a snack after nine holes. A peanut butter sandwich, apple, and protein bar are good examples of some of the best snacks.

Other important items are at least 12 golf balls, golf towel, tees, ball markers, golf glove, umbrella, divot repair tool, and sharpie marker to mark your name or initials on the ball and to keep score.

- Sunscreen
- Water bottle
- Snacks such as protein bar, pb & j sandwich, apple, banana
- Tees
- Divot tool
- Golf towel
- Golf balls
- Golf glove
- Ball markers
- Pencil, sharpie marker

Tee Times

It is important to know that when you decide to play golf you will need a tee time reservation.

Tee Times	Player 1	Player 2	Player 3	Player 4
7:36 AM	Wagner	Dufner	Stewart	Mickelson
7:44 AM	Woods	Stricker	Payne	Webber
7:52 AM	Jones	Brown	Paschetto	Scadowski
8:00 AM	Morrison	Mraz	Budd	Moore
8:08 AM	Emory	Pearson	Baker	Hines
8:16 AM	Gibson	Gabert	Harper	Hayes
8:24 AM	Hoffman	Scott	McCoy	Doe
8:36 AM	Sneider	Powell	Geneva	Pilot
12:00 PM	Earley	McIlroy	Sanders	Brock
12:08 PM	Fitzgerald	Mitchell	Wright	Williams
12:16 PM	Petty	Bryant	Martin	Jones
12:24 PM	Cruz	Griffin	Garcia	Clark
12:36 PM	Gordon	Diaz	Lopez	Robinson
12:44 PM	Black	Marcial	Hill	Thomas
12:52 PM	Tanner	Stevens	Young	Jackson
1:00 AM	Tucker	Green	Allen	Anderson

The reservation will guarantee you a spot on the course for the day and time you would like to play. Usually you need to make your tee time reservation at least 3 to 7 days in advance of the day you would like to play.

You will also learn of any daily rules and conditions for the course and can learn the weather forecast, especially when storms are predicted for the day.

Game formats

Scramble

Each player plays a tee shot, best shot is then selected, then everyone plays from that spot. Format continues until ball is holed.

Best ball

Only the best hole score between 2-4 players is used. One, two or even three best balls of 4 players can be used.

Modified Stableford

A point game where points are allocated for eagles, birdies, pars, and points are deducted for bogies and higher.

Medal play

Total stroke score for the round is counted.

Match play

A hole by hole win or lose competition.

Skins game

Lowest score on a hole wins or else carried over to next hole.

Nassau

A competition of two nine hole matches and a third match based on the difference between the two nine hole matches. If Billy is two up on the front nine and Joe is one up on the back nine, Billy wins the third match or Nassau one up.

The teeing ground

You begin every hole on the teeing ground. This is the flat area with several sets of tee markers identified by various colors. The colors of the tee markers will vary from course to course.

The front tee markers (closest to the hole) are for beginners. The middle set is for intermediate skilled players and the back tees are for advanced players.

Juniors just starting the game should always begin from the front tees or if you're under 10 years old you should begin even closer to the hole; from the yardage markers located in the fairways.

If you are under 10 years old you should play the par 3's from 100 yards away from the hole, par 4's 150 yards away and par 5's at 200 yards away from the hole.

Look at the diagram on page 242 for locations of teeing areas.

Ready golf

'Ready Golf' is a term that means you may play your shot as soon as you are ready to play. The rules of golf say that the player farthest from the hole always plays his shot before the others. However, juniors and beginners usually take lots of shots which take a lot of time and, therefore, to save time we don't always follow the farthest player always plays first rule. As long as you are not endangering anyone's safety or playing tournament golf rules you can save lots of time for the group by playing 'ready golf '.

Pre-shot routine

Along with playing ready golf is a good pre-shot routine that doesn't take a lot of time. A pre-shot routine is a series of steps that you take before playing your shot.

A good pre-shot routine takes less than a minute.

- Select the club you want to use.
- Take one or two practice swings.
- Address the ball with a good set up.
- Play your shot.

Beginners often take too many practice swings, this will slow down your group and you will also get very tired by the time you get to the last few holes. So playing at a good pace saves energy, especially if it is really hot outside.

You always need to be moving toward your shot and selecting your club while others are playing. This is important to playing at a good pace for the whole group, which is discussed next.

Pace

An important part of playing on the course is playing at the proper speed or pace in relation to the group playing in front of your group.

Golfers play in groups of up to 4 players and as a group you all need to continue moving along at a pace that "keeps you in touch" with the group in front of you.

You will tee off on the first hole about 10 minutes behind the group in front of you. Therefore, you should finish about 10 minutes after that group on the final hole you play.

Play quickly and safely

You only play your shot once the group in front is well out of the way and won't be in danger of being struck by your golf ball.

Once they putt out and replace the flagstick continue to wait until they are well off the green. Then you may play your shot to the green.

Keep in touch

You never want to have an entire hole open with no players on it in front of you when the course is crowded. As juniors you are just beginning and learning golf. You will probably be taking lots of shots and often looking for your golf ball in the trees or long grass.

Lost ball

It is important not to take too much time in looking for your ball because it will also slow down play for all the groups playing behind you. Take no more than 2 minutes to look for a ball. Also, use an old ball that you don't mind losing on holes with lots of water hazards or a forced carry to get over a lake or stream.

Whose turn is it?

The rules of golf say that the person farthest from the hole should always play first. However, as a beginner in golf and with the importance of keeping pace with the group in front it will be a big time saver to sometimes hit once you are ready to play even though you are not "away".

Perhaps the player furthest from the hole is looking for their ball or has to walk all the way across a fairway to get to their ball while you are already at your ball. Play your turn only if everyone is out of your way.

So use ready golf and save time and keep pace with the group in front of yours.

Keeping score

Take a look at this scorecard; there are lots of numbers and boxes.

Hole	1	2	3	4	5	6	7	8	9	Out
Gold Tees	235	515	385	185	320	440	410	432	555	3477
Blue Tees	230	505	373	173	304	415	400	426	539	3365
White Tees	210	485	353	153	284	395	380	406	519	3185
Handicap	11	13	9	17	15	3	7	1	5	
JON	4	5	6	5	4	7	4	7	5	
Chris	6	7	4	4	6	5	3	6	7	
Nick	7	4	5	3	6	5	4	7		
PEP	3	8	5	4	5	5	4	5		
Par	3	5	4	3	4	4	4	4	5	36
Handicap	15	13	11	17	9	5	3	1	7	
Red Tees	190	435	331	141	280	355	370	380	489	2971

Date: Scorer:

Hole number

At the top of each scorecard will usually be the hole number.

Yardages

Directly underneath each hole number will be the yardages of the holes from each of the different yardage markers.

Which yardage should you play?

If you are 6-8 then you should begin playing from the 150 yard marker located in each of the fairways of the par 4 and 5's and from 100 yards or less on par 3 holes.

If you are 9-11 you will play the most forward set of tees and with the shortest yardage. The tee markers are usually red for this set of tees but they can actually be any color and decided by the golf course people.

At age 12 and with some golf skills you can begin to move back a set of tees.

Handicap

Underneath the yardages are 'handicap'. This is a rating order of the difficulty of all the holes. The number 1 handicap hole is rated as the most difficult hole on the course and the number 18 handicap hole is the easiest hole on the course. Once you are comfortable playing golf you can use handicap strokes to fairly play a match against another player.

Say, for instance, you are playing your friend Nick. Nick averages about 4 shots better than you for 18 holes of golf. So if you wanted to have a fair match against Nick you could take 4 handicap strokes on the four toughest holes.

So you determine the 4 toughest holes by using the 1-4 hole handicap ratings on the scorecard. On those holes Nick would give you a stroke off your hole score, so for instance, if you and Nick both make a 5 on a hole where you get a stroke, you would then subtract a stroke and receive a 4 and then also a win for that hole.

You could determine the winner of the match by either the total score at the end minus 4 strokes or by determining the win or loss for each hole and whoever has the most hole wins is the winner of the match. Most juniors don't really need handicaps until later but it is always good to know the basics of how it is used.

Par

The next listed item is the par for each hole on the course. Par can be a 3,4,or 5 and is determined by the length of the hole. A short hole is a par 3, a medium length hole is a par 4, and a long hole is a par 5.

Par is always a good score for a hole. Remember, that each time you swing at the ball it counts as one stroke. You need to remember each stroke for the hole you play and then you will write down your score for the hole after you complete the hole.

When to write your score

Never write your score while still on the green as players behind you may be waiting to play up to the green and you don't want to slow down play for anyone. A good time to write your score is on the next tee.

Player name

Underneath the handicap and par numbers are the empty boxes for the names of each player and then all the hole scores following the player's name.

Front nine/back nine

After the first nine which is called the front nine holes you will add up all your hole scores and write the total in the 'Out' box. Then after the second nine which is called the back nine you will write the total of your back nine scores in the 'In' box. Then you add the two nine hole scores together for your 'Total' 18 hole score.

More info

The scorecard will also usually have lots of useful rules and advice and sometimes a map of each hole. This information is especially useful when playing a course for the first time.

Golf ball art

Golfers play in groups of up to four players per group. This means there could be up to four balls on the hole at the same time. It is always important to make sure you always play your own personal ball for each shot and not the ball of any of the other players.

A fun way to always identify your ball so you never hit anyone else's by mistake is to personalize all your balls with your own creative artwork. You can use a permanent Sharpie marker and create your own unique artwork or even just write your initials or name on your ball. This will help you and all others in the group identify and play your own balls throughout each hole. Have fun with it!

Take care of the course

It is important to know how to take care of the golf course while you are playing. Here is an easy checklist of the important things to remember.

The greens are the most important and delicate areas to maintain. Walk carefully on the greens so you do not scuff or ruin the delicate grass. Never run or drag your feet. Never step directly on the hole.

Only use the putter on the green. Never hit a ball with a full swing from a putting green.

Fix ball marks on the green with a divot tool.

Rake the bunkers when you finish playing from them. Walk in and out of bunkers from the low side and don't enter in from the high lip.

Fix your divot when you tear up the turf with your irons. Either replace the divot or fill with divot sand if provided on your cart

Avoid taking practice swings that tear up the turf.

Wear proper golf shoes or sneakers. Do not wear soccer or baseball cleats, or boots with big treads that can damage the greens.

Good Sportsmanship

Good sportsmanship means having good behavior, proper manners, and respect toward others and the golf course. It is always good to display good sportsmanship toward the other players in your group while you play on the course. Good sportsmanship allows everyone to play their best golf while also letting them enjoy their playing time with each other.

Some examples of good sportsmanship are complimenting others on their good shots, being helpful in assisting others in searching for lost golf balls, being quiet, still, and out of the way so others can concentrate during their shots, and generally being helpful in any way during the round of golf. Just helping out in any way whenever you can such as attending the flagstick on long putts and replacing the flagstick back in the hole after the others have finished putting are just some examples of good sportsmanship.

Also, a good sport can handle losing a match and, win or lose, will always shake hands and compliment their opponent after the match.

Poor behavior

Some examples of bad sportsmanship are talking, moving, or practice swinging while others are trying to play, getting angry, throwing or slamming clubs after bad shots, laughing at the bad shots of other players, damaging the course in any way, and not shaking hands after a game.

Self control

Another big aspect of good sportsmanship is to control your own temper and emotions when you are not playing your best golf. You should never display a bad temper by slamming or throwing your club in anger as this is very dangerous to the safety of others, yourself, damages the course, and distracts others from being able to play their shots.

At the finish of a round shake the hands of the other players in your group on the 18th green and tell them you enjoyed playing with them.

Etiquette

Etiquette means having good manners and always showing consideration to others on the course.

Stand quiet, still, and out of the way from other players while they play.

Play at a good pace and keep up with the groups in front of you.

Play safely so no one will ever be in danger from your swing or shot.

Be ready to play when it is your turn. This means, be at your ball, decide which club to use, read your putt.

Golfers should play with honesty, obey the rules, and play with good sportsmanship.

Count your clubs

Always count your clubs before and after playing golf. First, count your clubs before you leave your house so you are sure they are all in your golf bag before you leave home. If you practice your putting in the house or chipping in the back yard you can easily leave one club behind unless you make it a habit to always count your clubs before leaving your home. Then once you finish playing golf immediately count your clubs again before leaving the course. When you take both a wedge and putter to the green it is very easy to forget and leave a club behind.

You should put your name, phone number, and address on your clubs using address labels or you can have some shaft labels specially made with your name. You can put them around the shaft under the grip and then wrap some clear tape around to protect and hold the label securely.

Shot shapes

Golf balls can curve in different directions while they are flying through the air. Some of the different directions for a right-handed golfer are named using the following terms.

The main reason the ball curves is where the clubface is pointing when it hits the ball. If the club face is pointing to the right of your target while striking the ball it will produce a shot that flies to the right or curves to the right with a slice.

When the clubface is pointing to the left of your target while striking the ball it will produce a shot that flies to the left or curves to the left

It is useful to be able to curve the ball to the left or to the right especially when you need to go around a obstacle such as a large tree or stand of trees around the corner of a dog leg hole.

Curving your ball on purpose is a more advanced technique that you should only learn once you are able to hit the ball solid and straight. Ask your PGA Professional if you should begin trying to curve the ball based on your current skill level.

Slice

A ball that starts left and curves way to the right.

Fade

A ball that curves only slightly to the right

Push

A ball that flies straight to the right

Pull

A ball that flies straight to the left.

Draw

A ball the curves slightly to the left

Straight

A ball that flies perfectly straight toward the target

For a left-handed golfer

All the above terms refer to shots that go in the opposite direction because they stand on the opposite side of the ball.

Therefore, a ball that curves way to the right is called a hook for a left-handed golfer. (It goes behind the way he is facing)

A ball that curves way to the left would be a lefty's slice. (It goes away from the way he is facing.

Your natural shot shape

Everyone who learns golf will eventually develop a natural shot shape to all his or her shots. This means that the ball will consistently curve the same way each time you hit the ball. You will either have a slight curve to the right or a slight curve to the left for most of your shots.

Once you develop a natural shot shape you will be able to allow for this predictable curve for all your shots.

The best shape for most of your shots will be either a little fade or a little draw (curves only about 10-15 yards at most). Too much curve and your shots will lose distance.

As you play your longer shots you will want to set up so that you allow for the natural shape to occur. so for a little fade (slight curve to the right) you might line up and aim a little left of your target and allow the ball to curve in towards your target.

For a slight draw (curve to the left) you will want to line up slightly to the right of the target and then allow the ball to settle in from the right.

Always try to play the entire round allowing for your natural shot shape to occur, as this is how you will be most consistent.

Your shot shape strategy

The driver, 3 and 5 woods, and 5, 6, and 7 irons will curve the ball the most because they create the most ball speed and spin. Ten or fifteen yards of curve is okay for these clubs.

A good strategy for the driver is to either tee your ball on the left side or the right side of the tee box depending on which way you curve the ball.

If you curve to the left, then you will want to tee your ball on the left side of the tee box and aim down the right side of the fairway allowing the ball to curve back to the middle of the fairway. If your ball doesn't curve as much as you predicted it would hopefully still be on the right side of the fairway.

If you curve to the right you will want to tee your ball on the right side of the tee box and aim down the left side of the fairway and hopefully curve it back into the middle of the fairway.

The 8, 9 irons and wedges will only curve two or three yards at most so you can play for much less curve. The best strategy for hitting these, and all irons is, to aim to the side of the flagstick that has the most green regardless of your curve. If the flagstick is located on the right side of the green, then aim your shot to the left of the flagstick or the middle of the green.

INDOOR PRACTICE & RAINY DAY FUN

There will be many times when you can't go outside to practice.

Sometimes you'll want to practice your golf but you just can't make it to the golf course. Maybe it is dark outside, maybe the weather is bad, or you just can't get a ride to the course.

You can still have fun and get better with your golf in and around your own home. Sometimes you can swing in the backyard or inside an empty garage.

Here are a couple drills and games you can try around the house.

Practice your putting

Try practice putting or making a putting course in your home. On a carpeted floor set up some holes using paper cups or make a horseshoe shaped cup from cardboard and then putt into it.

Putting mat

Also, having a putting trainer mat like the one shown is a great training aid. This mat teaches good clubface alignment by placing the clubface against the hash marks so you're always aiming the clubface correctly.

The long parallel lines are a guide to show you how far to swing the putter back and forth when you use a nice smooth tempo for the distance you are trying to go.

Rails

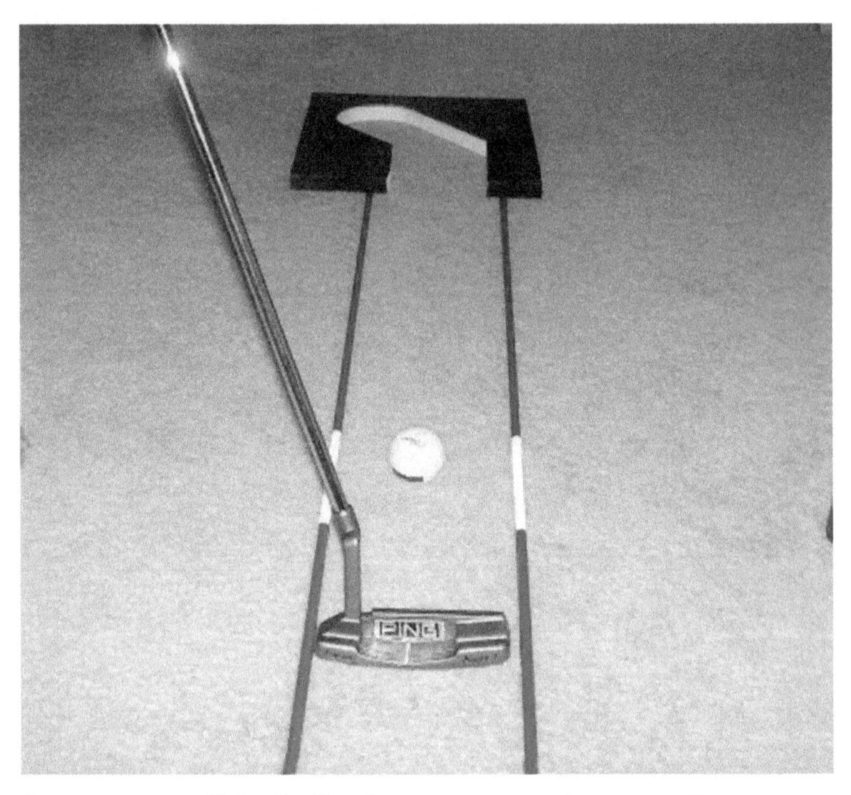

Set up two parallel rails like these or you can just as easily use some clubs for rails.

Practice putting keeping your putter in between the rails during your stroke to help you learn and maintain a good putting path.

Read golf books and magazines

There are many magazines about golf that can teach you about the different areas of the game. They are mostly published once a month and are a great way to stay up to date on the latest news and trends in golf.

You can read about the newest golf equipment and fashions, golf courses around the world, pro tournaments, golf tips, rules, as well as learn all about PGA and LPGA players and other influential golf people.

Golf Digest, Golf Magazine

Two of the best magazines for golf are Golf Magazine and Golf Digest.

It is always fun to get mail when you are a kid so ask your parents if you can earn an annual subscription to a golf magazine by doing some extra chores.

You can always visit your local library to read these magazines.

Exercise and work out

Almost all exercises are good. Using dumbbells, jumping rope, doing sit ups, push ups, riding an exercise bike, working out with stretch cords are all great ways to help increase your strength and get in good shape for golf.

Practice your setup position

in front of a mirror. Pick a PGA or LPGA Tour player and find a picture of him or her addressing the ball you can place next to you in front of a mirror. Each day try and copy their good set up by copying their posture, grip, stance, ball position, and with arms good and extended, etc.

Create an obstacle course

much like miniature golf that you have to putt through. Have a tournament with your friends and make score cards with the par for each hole and practice keeping score. Play an 18-hole tournament and add up your scores at the finish. Play over and over and try to improve your score each time.

Practice your swing tempo

You can swing a club in the back yard without hitting a ball to practice repeating the same tempo every time. You can practice making a full back swing and full follow through and into a full balanced finish position with all your weight on your left leg and body facing the intended target. You can practice making a good swoosh sound to get some speed at the ball. You can practice your pre shot routine and getting into your set up position.

Juggle

Juggling in golf is the ability to maintain the bouncing of a ball repeatedly off the clubface up and down without the ball falling to the ground. It is similar to a soccer player trying to keep the ball up in the air with only his feet.

Juggling is a fun exercise and it helps you learn clubface awareness and timing. It is very difficult to learn, so don't get frustrated if you can't do it at first.

In my experience of watching many juniors learn juggling it will take at least 6 months and maybe longer of frequent practice to learn juggling. So as a goal maybe you can try to learn juggling in only five months. Good luck!

Juggling will strengthen your grip and forearm and help with hand eye coordination while you are learning, which is always good exercise for golfers.

Visit websites

Golf websites are another great way to stay up to date on the latest current events, players, and golf equipment. Some of the best websites are:

- USGA.org
- Golf.com
- PGA.com
- PGATour.com
- Thegolfchannel.com
- MyTPI.com
- Titleist.com/my-game*
- AJGA.org
- Google your state name + junior golf to find out about junior golf groups in your area.

The next few pages show some of these web sites. There are lots more.

Some store websites for purchasing and learning about golf equipment are:

- Golfsmith.com,
- EdwinWatts.com,
- Amazon.com, and
- TGW.com.

*Go to the "Keep stats" section on page 208 for more about this website.

junior links

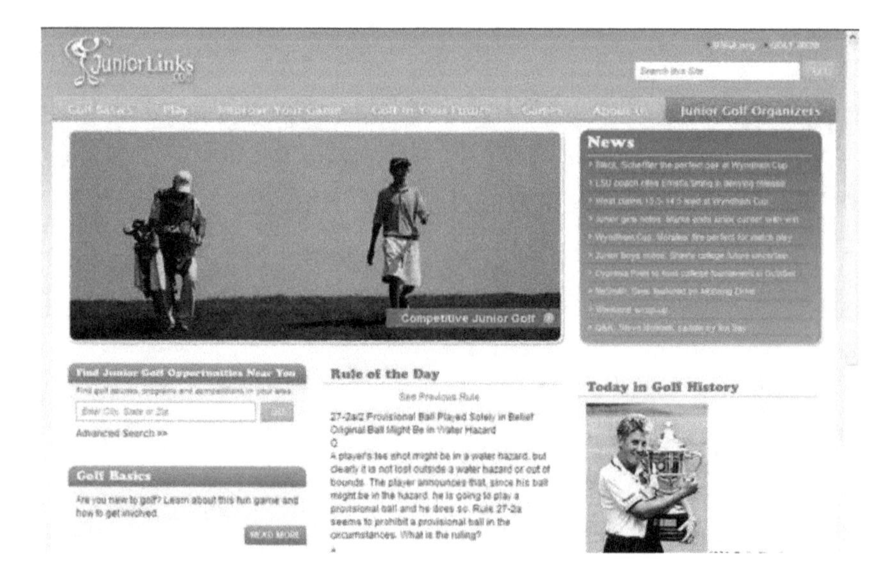

Golf.com

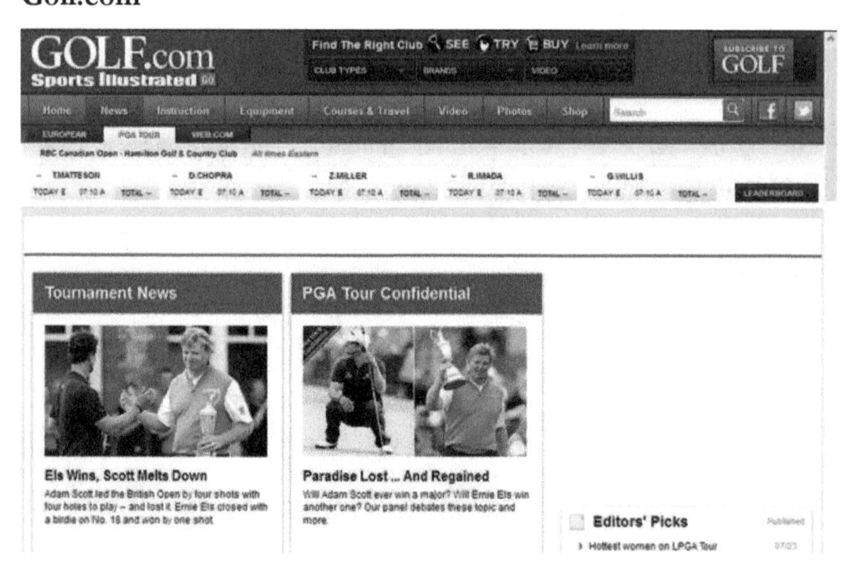

golfchannel.com

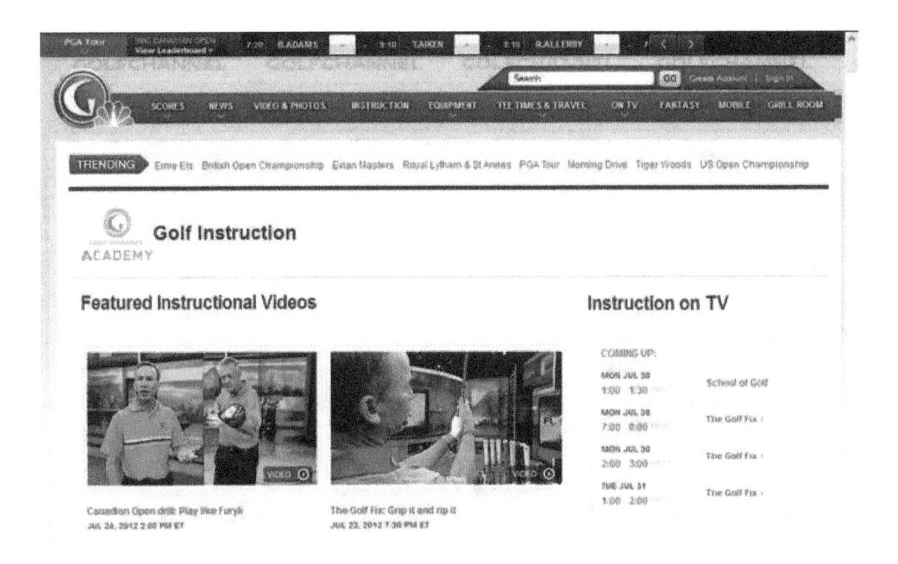

pga.com

mytpi.com

usga.org

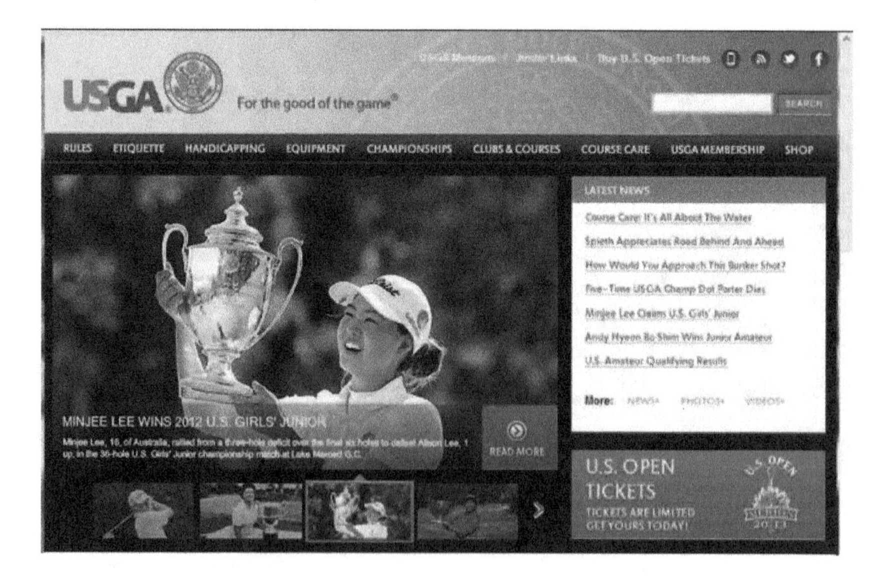

Play Wii Golf

Playing the Wii Golf video game on your television is a great way to learn the basics of golf.

You will learn such things as how to club yourself for hitting different distances, importance of proper alignment to the target, adjusting alignment left or right for different cross winds, proper order of play, adjusting swing length for short pitch shots, keeping score, and the risk versus reward for hitting shots of great difficulty over and toward hazards.

You also can compete against each other and against great PGA players and tour stars like Tiger Woods.

IMPROVING AND GROWING YOUR GAME

Work with a PGA professional

It is always helpful to have a professional golf instructor help you along if your parents can help support you for instruction.

Ask your parents if you can take lessons from a PGA Professional to help improve your skills. PGA Professionals are specially trained to teach golf and they will offer their trained eyes and experience to encourage you along in learning the fundamentals.

I recommend you listen carefully to your pro and take along a small notebook to write down all the key points from each of your lessons. Having a notebook entry of each lesson will be helpful as you can review each lesson often while practicing on your own time.

One lesson per month will allow you enough time to work on what you've learned and make it into a habit before moving on to the next month's lesson.

Whenever you practice you should try to work on some of the points from your lesson notebook. Try to get your golf lessons from one trusted PGA Professional and avoid getting tips from your friends.

Caddy

A caddy assists a player by carrying his clubs, assisting in club selection, keeps equipment clean and dry, and helps with the decision making that occurs throughout a golf round.

A great way to learn all about golf is by caddying. If your parents play golf, you can offer to caddy for one of them, or if you are at least 13 or 14 you can try and get a caddy job at a club that uses caddies. Not all golf courses will have caddies and most just use golf carts.

Caddies are usually only found working at private country clubs rather than the public golf courses. If you have a private country club nearby you can call out and ask for the caddy master and then ask him if there are caddy jobs available and that you would like to work as a caddy.

The caddy master oversees all the caddies and assigns them to a player as needed and will also train you in the beginning if you do not have any experience.

This is a great job to help you learn all that happens on the course and you will also earn a wage for working. And as a great bonus, caddies usually get to play the course for free in exchange for working.

Keep stats

A fun way to keep track of your golf improvement is to keep statistics of all your shots and scores. Statistics of your shots and scores each time you play will tell you what your game strengths and weaknesses are so you have insight into what areas to work on in order to improve.

Titleist.com/my-game on the Internet offers a free service where you can input all your course scores and statistics.

First, ask your parents if you can register and create a free Team Titleist account. Then, log onto Titleist.com/my-game.com and follow the directions to create a new account.

This is a free service and will set you up with an online account where you can post all of your golf scores and keep track of all your golf stats.

The statistics that you will be able to track are:

- score for each hole
- number of putts per hole
- number of fairways you hit with your tee shot
- sand saves (this is when you hit out of the sand onto the green and putt in the hole using only one putt)
- up and downs (chipping or pitching onto the green and using only one putt to hole the ball)
- greens in regulation (hitting onto a par 3 green with one shot, getting on a par 4 green with 2 shots, and getting on a par 5 green with 3 shots)

The program will create an overall average of all your statistics and scores and create trends in your game to help try and improve your game. You can print an advanced scorecard from the website which will have lots of boxes to input your statistics while you are on the course so you don't have to try and remember them until you get to your computer. Once you have a clear picture of your statistics try to work on improving in your weakest areas.

Usually chipping, pitching, sand, putting and driving are the weakest areas for juniors - and for all golfers! Team Titleist also offers video golf tips to help you in your weak areas.

Have fun using this service and try Titleist products whenever you can as they offer the very best equipment for golfers.

Compete with other juniors

Once you have learned many of the basics covered in this book, you will be ready to try competing against other junior players in tournament play. It is fun to take all that you have learned about golf and test your skills and abilities against other junior players in a tournament format.

Mostly, junior tournament golf is a wonderful learning environment and you will quickly learn through experience such areas as rules, sportsmanship, scoring, pace of play, etc. as well as improving your shot techniques. Learning golf is a long process so don't be frustrated if your skills are not equal to the skills of other juniors in the tournament. They may have been playing golf much longer than you or had more instruction. Use the experience of each tournament to learn and you will rapidly improve.

Remember that even in a professional PGA Tour golf tournament there is only one winner. Always concentrate on the process of hitting good golf shots and not on the outcome of always winning.

You can research online 'junior golf tournaments' near your city to see where and when tournaments are located near you.

The PGA section in your area will have a website with all the PGA junior tournaments for your area. Google "PGA Sections" to find your PGA section and then click on the link for the section(s) that includes your area.

The American Junior Golf Association (AJGA.org) and USKIDSGOLF.com also have many nationwide junior tournament schedules. The PGA Section tournaments and the AJGA tournaments are for 12-18 year old juniors. The U.S KIDS tour is for all ages under 15.

Attend PGA tournaments

Going to PGA Tour tournaments is a great way to watch and learn the methods of the very best players in the world.

You can watch in person their great consistency in ball striking and short game skills and then try to mimic their swings, techniques, and habits once you go to play golf.

Just being at the tournaments and studying these players will help you pick up the good habits of great players such as set up positions for each shot, swing tempo, pre-shot routines and lots more.

It is also fun to be a part of the crowd and cheer and watch the story of the tournament champion unfold.

GLOSSARY OF GOLF TERMS

A

Above the hole. On a sloping green, the high side of the green from where the hole is located.

Ace. When a player hits the ball directly into the hole from the tee with one stroke on a par three hole. Also called a hole in one.

Address. Taking your stance and placing the club head behind the ball. Addressing the ball. Grounding your club and taking your stance. In a hazard taking your stance alone as club cannot be grounded

Aim. Aiming the clubface at the target by 'squaring' it to the 'target line'.

Albatross. A hole played three strokes under par. A score of one on a par four hole. A score of two on a par five hole. Also called a Double Eagle.

Alignment. How the golfer lines up his shoulders, hips, feet, body and club head to the target line. Remember, the target line is the imaginary line drawn from the ball to the target.

All square. In match play a match is all square (tied) when both players or teams have won the same number of holes.

Angle of approach. During the golf swing this is the angle made between the ball and the clubface when the club strikes the ball. This angle affects how high the ball goes and the amount of 'backspin' put on the ball. The bigger the angle of approach the higher the ball flight.

The lower numbered clubs, Driver, 3 iron, 4 iron, etc. have lower angles of approach so the ball goes lower and travels farther.

The higher numbered clubs, 8 iron, 9 iron, pitching and other wedges have higher angles so the ball goes higher and doesn't travel as far.

Approach shot. A shot intended to land the ball on the green. The best place to hit your approach shots is from the fairway.

Apron. The short grass around the green that separates it from the surrounding fairway or rough. Also known as frog hair or fringe.

Army Golf. Hitting shots to the left and to the right instead of straight.

Attend (the flagstick). When a player has a long putt another player or caddie may hold the flagstick so the player who is putting can see where the hole is located.

If you attend the flagstick for another player you must remove it before the ball gets to the hole. It is a penalty if the ball strikes the flagstick while it is being attended.

It is a penalty if the ball hits the flagstick when putting a ball that is on the green.

Away. Describing the golfer whose ball is farthest from the hole. The player who is away should usually play first.

B

Back nine. The last nine holes of an 18-hole golf course. The back nine is also called the inward nine.

Backspin A golf ball spins when it is hit. The direction of the spin determines the 'flight path' of the ball. A backwards spin causes the ball to go up in the air.

Backswing. That part of the swing starting from the ground and going back behind the head.

Ball mark. A mark made by a ball landing on green. If the ground is hard the mark will be a small dent. If the ground is soft it will make a deep, large hole. You should always repair your ball marks.

Ball-marker. A token or a small coin used to mark the ball's position on the green. It is placed directly behind the ball so the player can lift the ball to clean it or get it out of another player's way and then replace the ball exactly where it was before he lifted it.

Ball-washer. Device found on many tees for cleaning golf balls.

Banana-ball. A shot made by a right handed player that curves to the right in the shape of a banana. Also called a 'slice'. A left handed player's banana ball 'slices' to the left.

Bare Lie. When the ball lies directly on hard ground without any grass to hold the ball up.

Below the hole. On a sloping green it is the low side of the green from where the hole is located.

Best ball. A form of team play using two, three, or four person teams. The team score on each hole is the lowest score made by one of the team members.

Let's say that Jon, Chris, Beth and Nick are playing as a team and they are playing a par four hole. Jon makes a 5, Chris makes a birdie 3, Nick makes par 4 and Beth makes a 5.

The team score for that hole is a 3. It is the best score of the four.

Birdie A hole played in one stroke under par.

Bite. A ball hit with a lot of backspin which makes it stop quickly instead of rolling when it lands. Depending on where the ball lands it may even roll backwards.

Blade. (1) A type of iron where the weight is distributed evenly across the back of the club head as opposed to mostly around the edges (see "cavity back").

Blade. (2) A poor golf shot when the bottom of an iron hits high up on the golf ball causing a low ball flight with a lack of control. Sometimes called a 'thin' hit.

Blast. A bunker shot that sends the ball and accompanying sand (hopefully) onto the green. Also known as an "explosion".

Blind shot. There are times when you must hit a shot where you don't see the landing area such as onto an elevated green from a lower teeing area.

Bogey. A hole played one stroke over par.

Break. When a putt does not roll in a straight line to the hole it is called a 'breaking' putt. The main reason is that greens are not perfectly flat and level and when you roll a ball on an uneven surface it does not go in a straight line.

Before you make a putt you have to look at the green and figure out the 'line' the ball will follow to the hole based on the slopes of the green and the speed of the putt.

As you get experience putting you will get better at 'reading' the greens.

Bump and run. A low shot that is intended to get the ball rolling along the fairway and up onto the green. Similar to a chip shot, but played from a greater distance.

Bunker. A dug out area that contains a layer of sand is called a sand bunker. Also called a "sand trap". It is considered a 'hazard' under the Rules of Golf.

There are special rules for playing from a hazard. We'll cover these later.

Bunker, Greenside. A bunker located next to or even in a green.

Bunker, Fairway. A bunker located on or in the fairway.

Bunker, grass. A bunker that has grass growing in it instead of having a layer of sand. It is not played as a hazard.

C

Caddy or Caddie. A person, often paid, who carries a player's clubs and offers advice. Players are responsible for the actions of their caddies. Players cannot receive advice from anyone other than their caddy or partner.

Carry. How far the ball travels through the air. Opposite of "run" which is how much the ball rolls out on the ground.

Cart. A small, four-wheeled electric or gas-powered vehicle used to carry players and their equipment around the golf course.

Also, a hand or electric powered (2-wheel) or 3-wheel) cart for carrying a bag of clubs.

Casual water. Puddles and wet ground resulting from rain, sprinklers, leaking pipes, sprinkler heads, and other sources. Snow and ice can also be taken as 'casual water', as well as water that overflows the banks of existing water hazards.

You are allowed to remove and drop your ball outside the area of casual water without penalty.

Cavity back irons. This type of iron is hollowed out in the middle of the back leaving more weight around the edges.

Chip. A short shot (typically played from very close to and around the green), that is intended to travel through the air over a very short distance and roll the remainder of the way to the hole.

Chunk. A swing that results in the club head hitting the ground before the ball, resulting in a large chunk of ground being taken as a divot. Also called a "fat" shot, or "chili-dipping".

Closed face. When in relation to the target-line the clubface is angled toward the player's body.

Closed stance. When a player addresses the ball with his/her front foot set closer to the target-line than his/her other foot. This player might be trying to draw the ball or to prevent a slice.

Club head. The 'business' end of the golf club.

Clubface. The front surface of the club head. Striking the ball with the center of the clubface increases distance and accuracy.

Clubhouse. This is where your golf day begins and ends. The clubhouse is a source for information about local rules, condition of the course, upcoming events and other useful information. You can usually purchase balls, clubs, clothes, and other golfing stuff in that part of the clubhouse used for the pro shop.

Compression. The measurement for expressing the hardness of a golf ball. Harder balls are intended for players with faster 'swing speeds' but may be useful in windy conditions for golfers with slower swing speeds.

Course. Area of land on which golf, and only golf, is played.

Course Rating. Course rating is a numerical value given to each set of tees at a particular golf course to approximate the number of strokes it should take a 'scratch' golfer to complete the course.

Cross-handed grip. The hands are placed in positions opposite that of the conventional grip. For right-handed golfers, a cross-handed grip would place the left hand below the right. Also known as the "left-hand low" grip, it has been known to help players combat the yips.

Cut. The reduction in the number of players during a multiple round stroke play tournament. The cut is usually set so that a fixed number of players, plus anyone tied for that place, or anyone within a certain number of strokes of the lead will participate in the subsequent round(s). Tournaments may have more than one cut.

Cut shot A shot similar to a fade. A cut curves from left to right (for a right-handed player), but is generally higher in trajectory.

D

Dimples. The round indentations on a golf ball cover which are used to help the ball make a steady and true flight. By reducing drag dimples allow a golf ball to stay in the air for a longer flight than would be possible with a smooth ball.

Divot. The chunk of grass and earth dug up during a stroke.

Dogleg. A left or right bend in the fairway.

Double bogey. A hole played two strokes over par.

Double eagle. A hole played three strokes under par. Also called an Albatross.

Downswing. The motion of swinging a club from the top of the swing to the point of impact.

Draw. A shot that, for a right-handed golfer, curves to the left; often played intentionally by skilled golfers. An overdone draw usually becomes a hook.

Drive. The first shot of each hole made from an area called the 'tee box'.

Drop Area. An area marked off where you drop and play a ball after hitting into a hazard.

Duck-hook. A severe low hook that barely gets airborne.

Duff. Also known as Dub. A horrible shot.

E

Eagle. A hole played in two strokes under par.

Equitable stroke control. The highest score you are allowed to take on a hole when you turn in your score for handicap purposes. 0- 9 hdcp - double bogey, 10-19 hdcp - 7, 20-29 hdcp - 8, 30-39 hdcp - 9, 40 up - 10.

Even. Having a score equal to that of par.

Explosion. A bunker shot that sends the ball, and accompanying sand, (hopefully) onto the green. Also known as a "blast".

European Tour. One of the world's leading professional golf tours along with the PGA Tour. Based in Europe, but also co-sanctions the major championships and World Golf Championships in the United States along with many other tournaments in Asia, Africa and Australia.

F

Fade. A shot, for a right-handed golfer, that curves slightly to the right and is often played intentionally by skilled golfers. An overdone fade will appear similar to a slice.

Fairway. The area of the course between the tee and the green that is well maintained allowing a good lie for the ball

Fairway markers. Fairway markers show the distance from the marker to the center of the green. Some fairway markers have the yardage written on them, but most are painted different colors for different yardages.

The most common colors used are: yellow=250 yards, blue=200 yards, white=150 yards, red=100 yards.

These colors are not standard and may change from course to course.

Fat. Hitting it 'fat' means the club makes contact with the turf before the ball resulting in poor contact and a big loss of distance.

Flagstick. A tall marker, often a metal pole with a flag at the top, used to show the position of the hole on a green. Also called the "pin".

An additional smaller flag, or other marker, is sometimes positioned on the flagstick to show the location of the hole (front, middle, or back) on the green.

Sometimes different color flags might be used to show the location of the hole.

Flier. A type of lie where the ball is in the rough and grass is likely to become trapped between the ball and the clubface at the moment of impact.

Flier lies often result in "flier shots", which have little or no spin (due to the blades of grass blocking the grooves on the clubface) and travel much farther than intended.

Flop Shot. A short shot, played with an open stance and an open clubface, designed to travel very high in the air and land softly on the green.

The flop shot is useful when players do not have "much green to work with", but should be attempted only when you have a good lie. Phil Mickelson is a master of the flop shot.

Fore. A warning shout given when there is a chance that the ball may hit other players or spectators.

Fringe, collar. A two to 3 foot border surrounding a putting green with grass similar to fairway.

Front nine. Holes 1 through 9 on an 18-hole golf course.

G

Gimme. A ball so close to the hole that your playing companions allow you to pick up your ball without putting. A gesture of sportsmanship. It still counts as a stroke for your score on that hole.

"Gimmes" are not allowed by the rules in 'stroke' play, but they are often given in casual matches.

A player in match play will generally concede a tap-in or other short putt by his or her opponent.

In match play, either player may formally concede a stroke, a hole, or the entire match at any time and this may not be refused or withdrawn.

Go to school. To learn from another player's putt or shot before your turn.

If another player putts before you and is on a similar line you have a chance to see how much break there is and how hard to hit the ball to get to the hole.

If another player hits a shot first you have a chance to see what club selection they use to go a certain distance.

Golf ball. A ball approved for play by the United States Golf Association. All golf balls must be the same size, but many other changes are permitted. 1.62 ounces, 1.680 inches in diameter.

They can be different colors. They may have more or fewer 'dimples' arranged in different patterns on the surface of the ball. Some balls have hard covers, some have soft covers. The insides are made from different materials. Some are a little heavier than others.

Golf ball makers are always trying to make a better golf ball within the rules made by the United States Golf Association. (USGA).

Golf club. Golf club has three possible meanings.

(1) It's a golf club. You use it to play the game. A player is allowed to carry up to fourteen (14) clubs during a round of golf.

(2) It can also mean a group of golfers who have formed a club to play golf.

(3) It's a golf club. It's the place where you play the game.

This would include the golf course, club-house, pro-shop, practice areas, etc. It could be a private, member's only golf club or a public course. A private course for members' and their guests only is a "Country Club".

If you see CC after a course name it is a Country Club. If you see GC after a course name it is a course open to the public.

Grain. The direction in which growing grass leans, usually towards the setting sun. On the greens it might change the way the ball rolls.

Depending on the kind of grass growing on the green and how the grass is cut, grain can be a big influence on the speed and movement of a putt.

Graduated rough, primary rough, secondary rough. When the grass is cut to different lengths. Usually, the further off the fairway the higher the grass.

Green. The area of specially prepared grass around the hole where putts are played.

Green in regulation (GIR). A green is considered hit "in regulation" if any part of the ball is touching the putting surface and the number of strokes taken to get it there is at least two less than par.

You have made a GIR if you hit a par 3 green in one stroke, if you hit a par 4 green in two strokes, and if you hit a par 5 green in three strokes.

Grip. Where you hold the golf club. Grips are made of material that help you grip the club without your hands slipping when you swing.

GCSAA. The American professional association for golf course superintendents.

Goldie Bounce. When the ball strikes a tree deep in the rough and bounces out onto the fairway. Also known as a "members' bounce" if the player happens to be a member of that golf course.

Grounding the club. Touching the ground with the club. When you ground your club at address it means you are ready to play your shot. If the ball moves after you ground your club it is counted as a penalty stroke.

Grounding the club is prohibited in sand bunkers or when playing from any marked hazard. You must play your shot from a hazard without grounding your club.

Ground under repair (GUR). An area of the golf course that is marked in some way as being repaired. If a ball lands in an area marked "GUR" a free drop (no penalty) outside the area of repair is allowed

Grooves. The grooves on the face of a club are designed to make the ball spin. The width, shape and depth of the grooves are regulated by the Rules of golf.

H

Hacker. An unskilled golfer.

Handicap. Is a way to determine how well a golfer plays the game. The USGA has invented a system that uses your scores to give you a golfing report card. They take your best scores and do some addition, subtraction, division and multiplication to come up with a number.

The best players have the lowest numbers. On a normal day, a player with a 1 or 2 handicap is expected to play a par 72 golf course in only a couple of strokes over par. On a good day, the same player will turn in a score under par.

Amateur golfers' handicaps are often used to group players in tournaments so they are playing with others of similar ability. Higher handicaps play against other higher handicappers and lower handicaps play against other low handicappers.

Handicap index. The actual number the USGA handicap system gives a golfer. It is written as a number to one decimal place. This number is used to decide your handicap when you play different courses.

Hardpan. Hard, usually bare, ground.

Hazard. Every sand bunker is a hazard.

Lakes, ponds, streams, rivers, oceans on the course or around the course are water hazards and marked with special yellow or red markers and/or lines.

Special rules apply when playing from a hazard. You may not move your ball in a hazard. You may not touch the ground or water when you address the ball. You may not move any loose material.

If you hit your ball into a water hazard and cannot find it or play it you are allowed to drop another ball outside the hazard and add a penalty stroke to your score for that hole.

Hole. A circular hole in the ground, which is also called "the cup". The regular cup is 4.25 inches across.

Hole in One. Getting the ball directly from the tee into the hole on a par three with one stroke. Also called an "Ace"

Hook - duck hook. For a right-handed golfer this is a shot that curves sharply to the left. A left-handed player's hook would curve sharply to the right.

Hosel. The part of the club head where the club head connects to the shaft.

I

Inside the leather. The length of the putter shaft between the head and grip of the putter. In a friendly match golfers may agree that any putt within the leather is a 'gimmie'.

Interlocking grip. Grip style where (for right-handed players) the pinkie finger of the right hand is hooked around the index finger of the left.

Inward nine. The back nine holes of a golf course. So named because older courses were designed to come back "in" toward the clubhouse after going "out" on the front nine.

Iron. A club with a flat-faced solid metal head. A golfer usually plays with a set of nine or ten irons. Each iron is made to hit the ball a different height and distance.

Irons have numbers them that lets the player tell them apart. Irons are numbered from 1 to 9. Letters are also used.

PW, AW, GW, LW, SW are short for Pitching Wedge, Attack Wedge, Gap Wedge, Lob Wedge, and Sand Wedge. Most club makers leave off the W and just use the letters P, A, G, L, S.

Some wedges have the number of degrees of loft on the bottom instead of a letter. 54, 56, 58, 60 or similar. The higher the number the higher the club hits the ball.

A 1 iron hits the ball longer and lower than the other irons. A 60-degree wedge hits it higher and shorter than all the other irons. All of the clubs in between hit the ball different distances so that whatever shot you need to play there will be a club to do the job for you.

A player cannot have one of every iron in the bag because that would be over the fourteen-club limit. You must choose which are best for you depending on your golf experience and ability.

K

Knockdown. A shot made to keep the ball low in windy conditions.

L

Lag putt. A long putt made to try to get the ball close to the hole.

Lay-up. A stroke played to position the ball in a certain spot.

Let's say your ball is 100 yards from a water hazard that you have to cross to get to the green and the water hazard is another 100 yards wide. You would have to hit the ball more than 200 yards to get over the hazard safely. Most amateur players cannot make this shot.

Instead you 'lay up.' You hit a shot 75 yards and land 25 yards short of the water. Then you hit your next shot 135 yards to make sure you get over the hazard.

Lateral water hazard. Red-staked hazards on a course. Refer to the diagram at the end of the Rules section.

Lie (1) How the ball is resting on the ground. It could be on short grass in the fairway, deep in the rough, on bare ground, on an upslope, downslope or many other places. A good lie helps you make a good shot while a poor lie makes it harder to hit the shot you want to make.

(2) The lie of a golf club is the angle between the center of the shaft and the sole of the club head. You should play with clubs that have the correct lie for your height. Your PGA professional will help you with this.

Line. The path the ball it expected to take following a stroke.

On the putting green it is important to know your line and other players' lines on the green. If you step on another player's line it is considered really bad etiquette (manners).

Also, if you step in your line or your partner's line it is a penalty.

Line of the putt. The intended path of a putt to the hole

Links. A type of golf course, usually along a stretch of coastline. The earliest golf courses in Scotland were links courses.

Loft. The angle between the club's shaft and the club's face. The bigger the angle the higher the club will hit the ball. A three-iron angle might be 18 degrees. A wedge could be 60 degrees. All of the clubs between these would be three or four degrees different so they will each hit the ball different heights and distances.

Loose impediment. A small natural item such as a loose stone, stick or leaf, or clump of dirt which is not attached to something or growing, or stuck solidly in the ground, or stuck to the ball.

If it's not in a hazard players are generally permitted to move them out of the way, but if the ball is moved while doing so there is a one-stroke penalty.

M

Match Play. A form of golf play where players or teams compete against each other on a hole-by-hole basis.

Medal play. Style of play in which the player with the fewest strokes wins. Most professional tournaments are medal play. Also known as "stroke play".

Member's bounce. Any favorable bounce of the golf ball that improves what initially appeared to be an errant shot.

Mis-read. You mis-read a putt when it doesn't follow the line you thought it would.

Mulligan. You get to hit a shot over again without counting the first time you tried to hit it.

It is not allowed by the rules and not practiced in tournaments, but friends do it all the time when playing together.

It's not a good idea to play mulligans because it slows play and keeps other golfers waiting.

N

Niblick. Term used in the early days for a club like today's 9 iron. Google 'old names for golf clubs' to learn what clubs were named during the years before they were numbered and discover what you would be using if we still called some clubs 'spoons', 'mashies' and "mashie niblicks'.

Nine Iron. A club used to hit the ball very high for short distance shots.

O

One ball rule. You are not allowed to switch from one type of ball to another during a round of golf.

Open face. When the clubface is facing away from the player.

Open Stance. When a player addresses the ball with his front foot back further from the target line than his rear foot.

Outside Agency. Any person or animal not part of a match that interferes with a ball in play. A ball interfered with while in motion is played as it lies. If while at rest, then it is replaced. On a putting green a deflected ball must be replaced without penalty

Outward nine. The first nine holes of an 18-hole golf course. So named because older courses were designed to come back "in" toward the clubhouse after going "out" on the front nine.

Out of bounds. Areas that are not part of the golf course. If you hit a ball out of bounds you must play another ball from the original spot and add a one stroke penalty to your score for that hole.

Overlapping grip. See Vardon grip.

P

Pace. The speed at which a putt must be struck to get to the hole.

Pace and break are the two components of 'reading' a green.

Pace of play. How long it takes to play the game. A good pace of play is 3 1/2 to 4 hours for 18 holes.

Par. The scoring standard for each hole on the course. A golf course will have each hole as a par of 3, 4, or 5 as determined by the total distance in yards for the hole. Par for the course is the sum total of all pars for the course. Making a par for a hole or the entire 18 hole course is always a good score.

Birdie - one below par.

Bogey - one above par.

Eagle - two below par.

Double Eagle (Albatross) - three below par.

Ace - hole in one.

Double Bogey - two above par.

Triple bogey - three above par.

Quadruple Bogey - four above par.

Penalty. A stroke added to your score determined by the Rules of Golf.

PGA of America. The trade association of teaching pros and other golf professionals in the United States. The PGA:

- Promotes and grows the game.
- Manages/operates golf courses/ranges, pro shops.
- Teaches the game.
- Organizes tournaments.
- Trains its professionals.

Pin. Slang for "flagstick".

Pin-high. Refers to a ball on the green that is positioned along an imaginary horizontal line through the hole and across the width of the green.

Pitch. Short shot, typically from within 50 yards, usually played with a higher lofted club and made using a less than full swing. It is intended to flight the ball toward a target (usually the hole) with greater accuracy than a full iron shot.

Pitch mark. A divot on the green caused when a ball lands. Players must repair their pitch marks, usually with a tee or a divot tool.

Play it down. Once you hit the ball off the tee you are not allowed to touch it again until it's on the green.

Play through. Permission granted by a slow-moving group of players to a faster-moving group of players to pass them on the course.

Plugged Lie. Bad lie where the ball is at least half-buried. Also known as a "buried lie" or in a bunker a "fried egg".

Pop-up. Poor tee shot where the top of the club head strikes under the ball, causing it to go straight up in the air. In addition to being bad shots, pop-ups frequently leave white scuffmarks on the top of the club head, or dents in persimmon clubs. Also known as "sky shots".

Preferred lies, winter rules. You are allowed to lift, clean and place your ball, usually because of poor conditions as a result of bad weather.

Pre-shot routine. Are the steps an experienced player goes through to get ready for his or her shot. It usually involves taking practice swings and visualizing the intended shot.

Pro, Professional. A person who plays or teaches golf for financial reward. May also work as a touring pro in professional competitions and/or as a club pro.

Pro Shop. A shop at a golf club, run by the club professional, where golf equipment can be purchased

Pull, pull-hook. A poor shot played severely to the left as opposed to normal hooks that curve from right to left. A pulled shot goes directly left. A pull-hook starts left and then curves even more left.

Punch shot. A shot played with a very low trajectory, usually to avoid interference from tree branches when a player is hitting from the woods. Similar to the knock-down it can also be used to avoid high winds.

Push, push-slice. A shot played severely to the right as opposed to normal slices that curve from left to right. A pushed shot goes directly right. Similar to the "block". A push slice starts as a push to the right then slices even more right. Also, a term used in match play where neither competitor wins the hole.

Putt. A shot played on the green, usually with a putter.

Putting green. A closely mowed area around the hole.

Practice green. A green usually found close to the clubhouse used for warm up and to practice putting.

Putter. A special golf club with a very low loft that makes the ball roll.

Q

Q-School. "Qualifying School", a term used for the qualifying tournament on several major professional tours, such as the PGA Tour, European Tour, or LPGA Tour. Q-School is a multi-stage tournament (four for the PGA Tour, three for the European Tour, two for the LPGA) that culminates in a week-long tournament in which a specified number of top finishers (25 plus ties in the PGA Tour, 30 plus ties in the European Tour, and exactly 20 in the LPGA) earn their "Tour Cards", qualifying them for the following year's tour. The final tournament is six rounds (108 holes) for men and five rounds (90 holes) for women.

R

Range Finder. Golfers use small, hand held lasers to find the distance from the flagstick before hitting an approach shot.

Ranger. Person at the course who keeps play moving at a proper pace.

Ready Golf. Be ready to play when its your turn by figuring out your next shot while other players in your group are playing their shots or while you're walking to your ball.

Release. The point in the downswing at which the wrists uncock. A 'late' release is one of the keys to a powerful swing.

Rough. The grass that borders the fairway, usually taller and coarser than the fairway.

Rub of the Green. Occurs when the ball is deflected or stopped by a third party or object.

S

Sand save. When a player makes a score of two or less from a greenside bunker.

Sand trap. See bunker.

Sand wedge. A special club made for playing out of a bunker. The modern sand wedge was invented by Gene Sarazen, a member of the Golf Hall of Fame.

Sandy. (or Sandie) A score of par or better that includes a sand bunker shot. Sandies are counted as points in some social golf games.

Scramble. When a player misses the green in regulation, but still makes par or better on a hole.

Also a two or four man format, similar to Best Ball, except in a scramble, each player strikes a shot, the best shot is selected, then all players play from that selected position.

Scratch golfer. A player with a 0.0 or lower USGA handicap. +1.0 is a lower USGA handicap than 1.0.

Shank. A horrible shot in which the golf ball is struck by the hosel of the club. A shanked shot will only go a short distance and usually slice or hook.

Short game. Shots that take place on or near the green. Putting, chipping, pitching, and greenside bunker play are all aspects of the short game.

Skin. A skins game pits players in a type of match play in which each hole has a set value (usually in money or points). The player who wins the hole is said to win the "skin" and whatever that skin is worth. Skins games may be more dramatic than standard match play if it is agreed by the players that holes are not halved (tied). Then, when any two players tie on a given hole the value of that hole is carried over and added to the value of the following hole. The more ties the greater the value of the skin and the bigger the eventual payoff.

Slice. A poor shot for a right-handed golfer that curves sharply from the left to the right. A shot that follows the same direction but to a lesser degree is referred to as a fade or a cut and is often intentional. The curved shape of the flight of the ball is a result of sideways spin. For that reason "slice" does not refer to a putt which "breaks".

Slope rating. The Slope Rating is a number, from 55 to 155, used to determine the level of difficulty of a golf course for a bogey golfer. An "average" course has a slope rating of 113. The higher the slope rating the more difficult the course.

Snap hook. A severe hook that usually goes directly left as well as curving from right to left. Also known by the somewhat redundant term "Pull-Hook".

Snowman. To score an eight on a hole. So-named because an eight (8) looks similar to the body of a snowman.

Sit. Telling the ball to drop softly and not roll after landing.

Speed. A term used to describe the pace of a putt. Proper 'speed' of a putt will either hole the putt or leave it about 18 inches beyond the cup.

Spray. To hit shots in a lot of different directions

Stimpmeter. A device used to measure the speed of putting greens.

Stroke Play. See Medal Play

Stymie. At one time you were allowed to block another player's putting path to the hole if your ball was in their line.

Stymies are no longer played. You must mark and lift your ball if it is in the way. You must even move your marker if your marker is in the way.

Sweet spot. The location on the clubface where the best ball striking results are achieved. The closer the ball is struck to the sweet spot the higher the power transfer ratio will be.

Swing. The movement a golfer makes with his/her club to hit the ball.

Swing speed. Is the speed, in miles per hour, of the club head through the hitting area when it makes contact with the ball.

T

Tap-in. A ball that has come to rest very close to the hole leaving only a very short putt to be played. Often recreational golfers will "concede" tap-ins to each other to save time.

Target-line. A imaginary straight line from the ball to its intended target and extended back past the golfer's rear foot.

Tee. A small wood or plastic peg placed in the ground upon which the golf ball is placed prior to the first stroke on a hole. May also refer to the teeing ground.

Teeing ground. The area from which you hit your drive or tee shot. The teeing ground for a particular set of tees is two club lengths in depth. The ball must be teed between the markers, called tees, that define the teeing ground's width and no further back than its depth. Tees are colored, but there is no standard for colors. The "teeing ground" refers to one set of tees. Most courses have at least three sets of tees and some have more than twice that many. The areas where tee markers are placed are called "tee boxes".

Tee time. When you arrange a time and day to play at a golf course you make a 'tee time'. Your tee time is when you are on the first tee ready to play.

Tempo. The smooth change of the speed of a player's swing from first movement to ball strike.

Ten finger grip. Grip style with all ten fingers on the club. Also known as the Baseball grip.

Thin shot. A poor shot where the club head strikes too high on the ball. When taken to an extreme it is known as "blading" the ball.

Through line. When putting, the imaginary path that a ball would travel on should the putted ball go past the hole. Usually observed by PGA players and knowledgeable golfers when retrieving or marking a ball around the hole.

Through the green. The entire area of the golf course, except for the teeing ground, of the hole being played. Includes the green of the hole being played and all hazards on the course.

Tips. The championship tees on a golf course are known as "the tips".

Topped. An errant shot where the club head strikes on top of the ball, causing the ball to roll or bounce rather than fly.

Trajectory. The curving flight of the ball as it leaves the clubface, rises into the air and then falls to the ground.

U

Unplayable. A player can declare his ball unplayable at any time when it is in play (other than at a tee), and can drop the ball either within two club-lengths no closer to the hole, or further from the hole in line with the hole and its current position, or where he played his last shot. A penalty of one stroke is applied. A ball declared unplayable within a hazard must be dropped within that hazard.

Up and down. Describes the situation where a player holes the ball in two strokes starting from off the green. The first stroke, usually a "pitch", a "bunker shot" or a "chip", gets the ball 'up' onto the green, and the subsequent putt gets the ball 'down' into the hole. A variation is called "up and in".

United States Golf Association (USGA). Governing body for rules of golf in the United States. The USGA:

- Conducts 13 national championships i.e. U.S. Open, U.S. Amateur U.S. Junior Am.

- Maintains equipment standards and tests equipment.
- Provides handicaps and course ratings.
- Does turf grass research.
- Preserves the history of the game.
- Has a golf museum.
- Provides grants and initiatives to introduce the game to people who otherwise wouldn't be able to play. $58 million since 1997.

V

Vardon grip. A common grip style in which (for right-handed players) the right pinkie finger rests on top of the left index finger. Also known as the "overlapping grip", it is named for Harry Vardon, a champion golfer of the early 20th century.

W

Water hazard. Yellow staked hazards on a course. Refer to the diagram at the end of the Rules section.

Wedges. Irons that have high lofts and are designed for short yardage shots.

Whiff. An attempt to strike the ball where the player fails to make contact with the ball. A whiff must be counted as a stroke.

Wood. Named because the head was originally made of wood. Drivers, fairway clubs and hybrids that now have metal heads.

Worm Burner. A shot that is hit low and hard.

Y

The yips. A tendency to twitch during the putting stroke. Some top golfers have had their careers greatly affected or even destroyed by the yips. Prominent golfers who battled with the yips for much of their careers include Sam Snead, Ben Hogan, and, more recently, Bernhard Langer.

Z

Zinger. A ball hit high and hard.

TYPES OF GOLF SHOTS

For right handed players

- Slice. A big curve to the right
- Hook, duck hook, turn it over. Big curve to the left
- Push. A shot that goes straight to the right
- Pull. A shot that goes straight to the left
- Fade, Cut shot. A slight curve to the right
- Draw. A slight curve to the left

For left handed players. All shot curvatures are opposite. For example, a lefties slice would be a big curving shot to the left.

For all players

Knock down shot. A low trajectory shot

Lob shot. An extremely high trajectory short shot

Explosion shot. Out of the bunker or deep rough –making a big swing with a very lofted wedge when there is a lot of sand or grass around ball to pop ball up in air

Top, Skull. A thin or bladed shot with the leading edge of the club head and not the clubface

Fat, Chunky, Chili dip. Hitting behind the ball with club head first

Whiff. To swing and completely miss the ball.

Lag putt. To get a long putt close to the hole

Die it in the hole. To hit a putt with such slow speed that it is able to fall in the side of the hole if it had to.

THE RULES of GOLF

The rulebook of golf has 34 rules. The United States Golf Association (USGA) and the Royal and Ancient Golf Club of St. Andrews in Scotland together write the rules. You can buy a rulebook for about two dollars and it is good to keep it in your golf bag. Also, www.USGA.org is a great website that lists the rules and they also explain many rules with video clips which makes learning them very quick and easy to understand.

Learning the rules takes a lot of time and explaining all of them would take another book! Juniors learning golf are not expected to know all the rules even as they play tournaments and the tournaments themselves are actually a learning ground to help you learn the rules. Whenever you have a question about a ruling you should always ask the PGA Pro after your round to help you with the correct decision.

Here are most of the rules you will need to learn explained in a simple list. The penalty for breaking rules can be to add one or two strokes to your score, disqualification when in a tournament, or loss of the hole when in match play. The rules also help you by providing relief in many situations so a basic knowledge of these listed rules can help you in many situations.

1. Each time you swing at the ball it counts as one stroke.

2. Match play is hole-by-hole play against another player. You win or lose a hole based on your score for that hole. If you make a 4 and your opponent makes a 6 you win the hole. The difference in amount of strokes does not matter, only that the hole is won or lost.

3. Stroke play is your total score for 18 holes.

4. The maximum number of clubs you can carry in your golf bag is 14, and you can always play with a set of less than 14 clubs. Penalty for too many clubs is to add 2 strokes for each hole you play with to many clubs. Maximum penalty is 4 strokes.

5. Play without delay. Keep pace with groups playing in front of you. Penalty for slow play is 2 strokes added to score.

6. The person with the lowest score on the last hole played is said to have the 'honor' and that person will tee off first on each tee box. When there is a tie on a hole then the order remains the same from the prior hole played. In stroke play there is no penalty for hitting out of turn. In match play, a player can be required to cancel the stroke played out of turn and replay the shot.

7. You must tee off from in between the tee markers on each hole. If you don't tee off from inside the markers then in match play you must re-tee and play another shot from within tee markers. In stroke play the penalty is two strokes and must be re-teed from inside markers.

8. You can have a maximum of 5 minutes to search for a lost ball.

9. The ball must be played as it lies. You are not allowed to improve your lie, move or clean your ball before playing it. Sometimes we agree to improve our lie if conditions on the course are not good usually because of wetness or poor grass conditions.

10. If your ball falls off the tee while addressing it and without swinging at it, there is no penalty and can be re-teed.

11. You may not ground your club (touch the ground before striking ball) in a hazard while taking your stance and set up. This includes all bunkers and water hazards.

12. You can attend a flagstick for someone when they are far from the hole, but you must remove it once they play their shot.

13. If you move your resting ball by mistake, you must replace it to its original spot and add one penalty stroke.

14. You must mark your ball (you can use a quarter or nickel as a marker) before lifting it on the putting green.

15. Whenever you have to drop your ball with a penalty or for relief you must hold it out at arm's length and shoulder height and drop it. You must re-drop it if it moves closer to the hole, rolls more than two club lengths from the spot where it landed, or rolls back in hazard or on cart path.

16. You can clean your ball once you mark it on the putting green, also when taking relief from casual water, relief from man made obstructions like a cart path or sprinkler head, or whenever you are

taking relief from a penalty situation such taking ball out from being stuck in mud in water hazard and taking penalty stroke to play from behind hazard.

17. You can move loose impediments (loose objects) such as pebbles, leaves, small sticks from around your ball or on your line of putt. You cannot let your ball move while you do this or it is a one-stroke penalty and the ball must be replaced.

18. Whenever you have to drop your ball with a penalty or for a relief situation you must hold it out at arm's length and shoulder height and then drop it. You must re-drop it if it moves closer to the hole, rolls more than two club lengths from the spot where it landed, rolls back in hazard or on cart path. When the ball rolls closer or farther than 2 club lengths after two drops you may place it with your hands at the spot where it first lands on the second drop.

19. You can take relief without penalty whenever your ball comes to rest on a paved cart path or onto any man made obstruction such as a sprinkler head. You find the nearest point of relief that is no closer to the hole and then drop.

20. You can take relief without penalty whenever your swing will come in contact with a man made obstruction such as a sign post, cart path or sprinkler head.

21. You can take relief without penalty whenever your ball comes to rest in casual water or if you would have to stand in casual water. Casual water is water that is not usually part of the course, such as after a rainstorm when puddles are formed in the fairways, greens, or putting greens. You find the nearest point of relief that is not closer to the hole and take a drop.

22. A ball in a water hazard (defined by yellow stakes and lines) can be played three ways. A water hazard is usually a pond or body of water that you must carry over to get to the hole 1. You can play it from within the hazard (only if possible). 2. You can replay from where you hit it from with a penalty of one stroke added to your score. 3. You can stay in line with the point where it crossed into the hazard and also in line with the flagstick and drop back as far back as you like with one penalty stroke added to your score.

23. A ball in a lateral water hazard (defined by Red stakes) can be played in 5 ways. A lateral water hazard can be a stream or body of water that is to the side of the hole and you are not usually forced to carry over. 1) You can play the ball from the hazard (if possible). 2) You can replay from the spot where you played your shot. 3) You can play from a point in line with the flagstick and behind the hazard as far back as you'd like to go. 4 and 5. You can drop within two club lengths either to the left or right side where it crossed the hazard line but no nearer the hole.

24 Ball lost or out of bounds. Out of bounds is defined by a white line or white stakes. A ball is out of bounds when all of it lies within the out of bounds lines. Whenever a ball is lost or out of bounds you must add a penalty stroke and then replay from the spot where you last played your shot. So if you hit from a tee box and the ball goes out of bounds or gets lost in some trees you must replay from the teeing area and you would then be playing your third shot.

25. Whenever there is a chance your ball may be lost or out of bounds you can play a provisional ball from the same spot where you just played. A provisional ball is another shot played from the same spot and will save you time from having to go back to where you just hit if your ball is indeed lost or out of bounds. It only becomes the ball in play once you determine that your first shot is indeed out of bounds or lost.

26. Ball Unplayable. Whenever your ball is in an unplayable lie you can take relief with the penalty of one stroke. An example of an unplayable lie when it is up against a tree and you are unable to swing to hit it. The 3 ways to play are 1. Play from the spot where you last played. 2. Drop within 2 club lengths no closer to the hole of the spot where ball is unplayable. 3 Keep the spot where the ball lies and drop back in line with the flagstick, going as far back as you would like so as to get a good shot.

27. When you are playing in a competition and are unsure how to play within the rules you can play an extra ball from a spot where you think you are entitled to play and then tell the rules committee immediately after the round in order to get a proper ruling.

WATER HAZARD

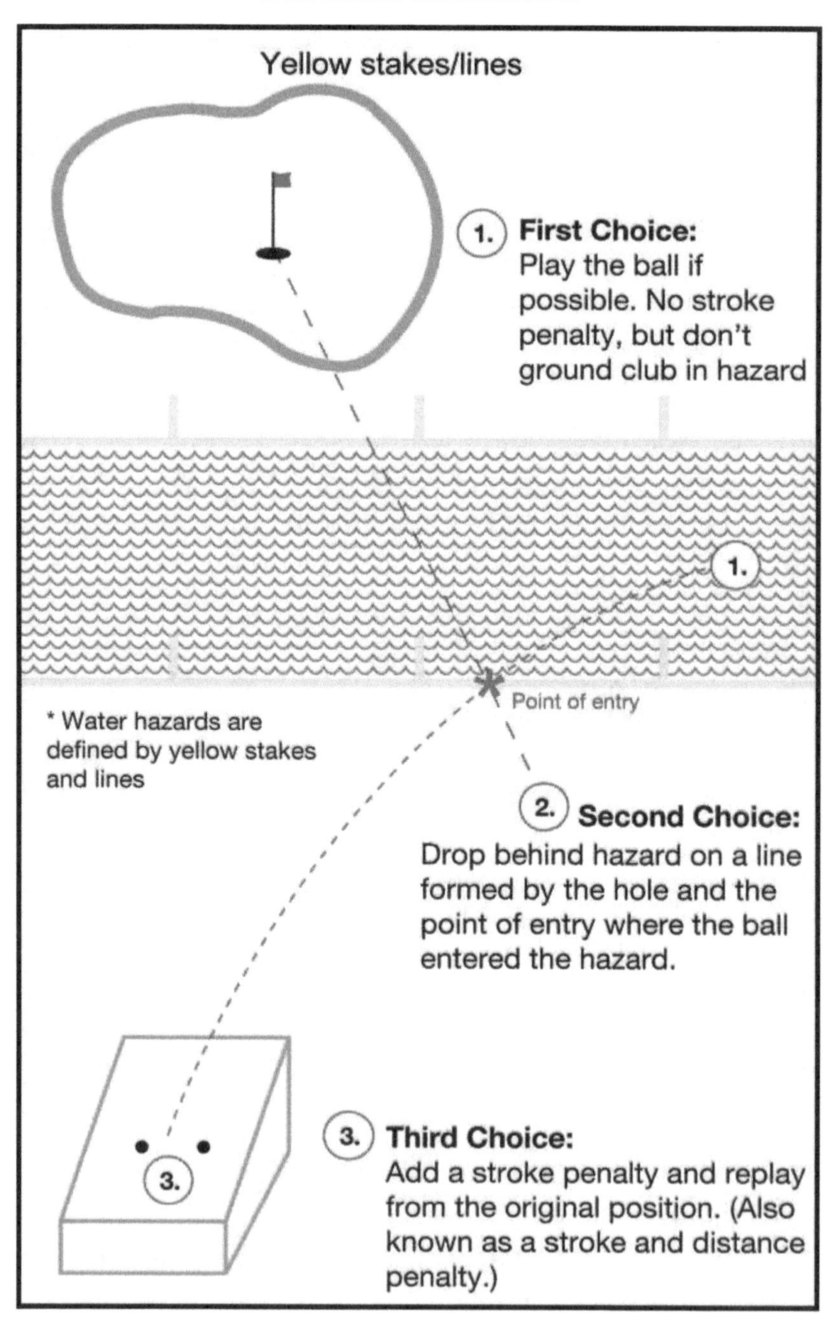

LATERAL WATER HAZARD

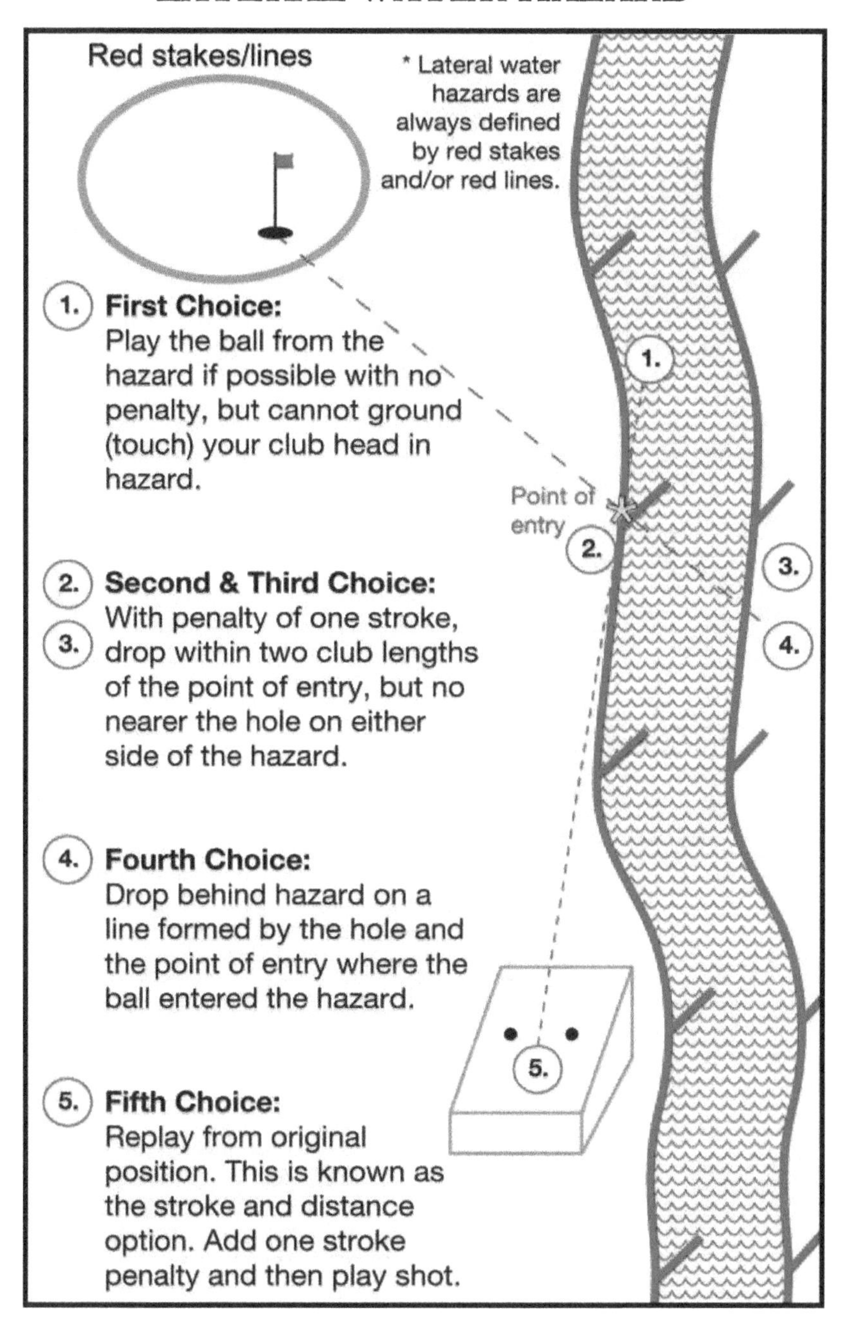

DOG LEG RIGHT

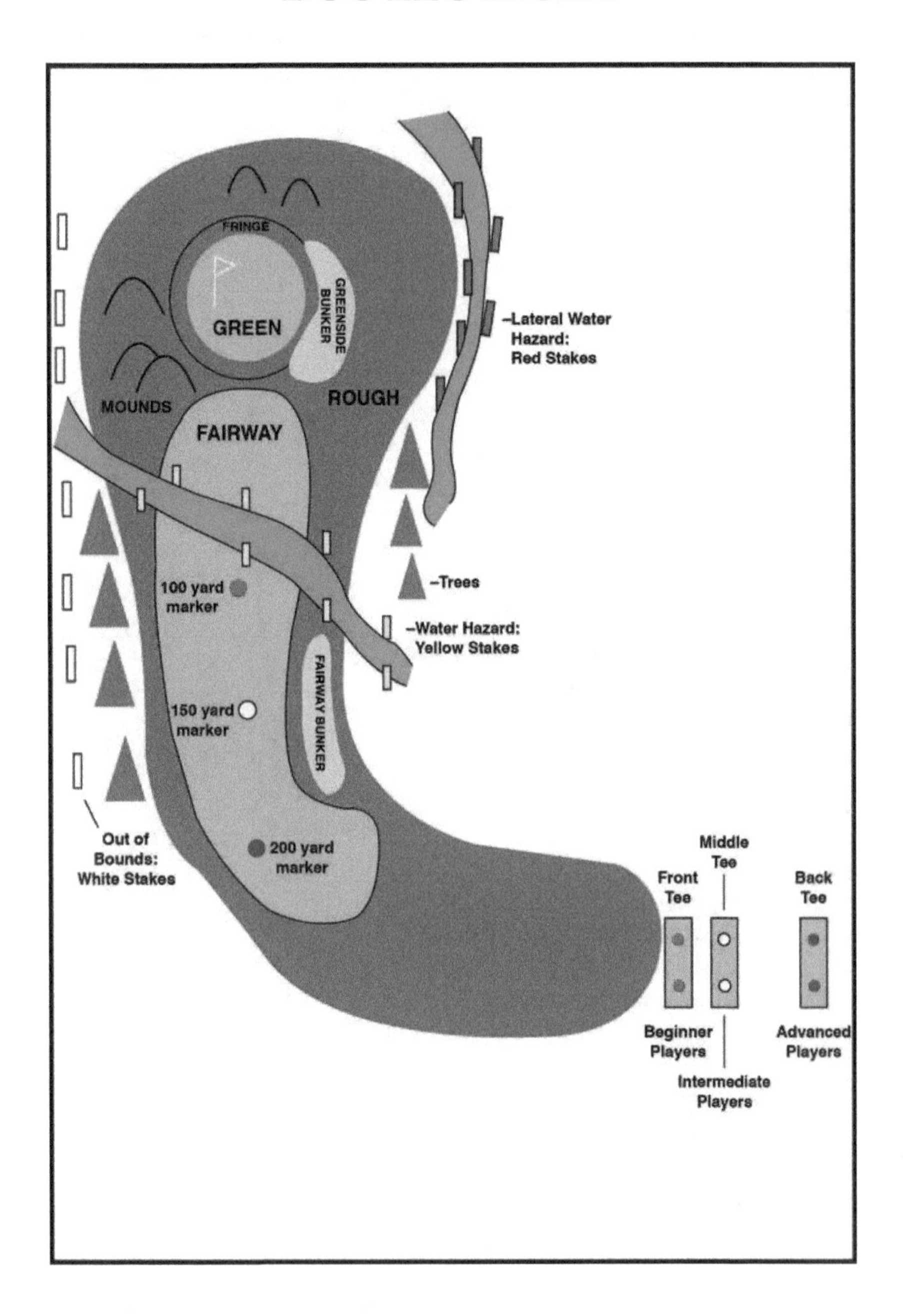

FUN GOLF FACTS

The youngest golfer to score a hole in one was Coby Orr at age 5 in 1975

Tiger Woods started playing golf when he was just 9 months old.

Tiger Woods made his first hole in one at age 8.

The first golf course was St Andrews, which is over 400 years old.

The first golf balls may have been made of wood. Then golf balls were made of strips of leather sewn and stuffed with feathers and used until the 1800's.

In 1971, astronaut Alan Shepard hit two golf balls 200 and 400 yards using a small one-armed swing, because of the lessor effects of gravity on the moon. On earth these shots would have gone just a few yards.

The longest drive in competition is over 500 yards long.

The longest putt ever made in competition is over 50 yards long.

The crow's nest is a small room that sits atop the Augusta National clubhouse and is where amateurs stay while playing in the Masters.

The oldest golfer to shoot his age was 103.

There are over 300 dimples on a golf ball.

Tour player Art Wall made 54 holes in one during his career.

The major tournaments in golf consist of 4 tournaments and are The Masters, US Open, British Open, and PGA Championship.

Jack Nicklaus holds the most major championship victories with eighteen.

Tiger Woods has fourteen majors as of 2012.

Winning all four majors in one year is called the Grand Slam.

In 1930, Bobby Jones won the Grand Slam, which, at that time, consisted of the US Amateur, British Amateur, US Open, and British Open

Tour player Byron Nelson won a record 11 tournaments in a row in 1945

Titleist is the most popular brand of golf ball.

The PGA of America, founded in 1916, is the largest sports organization in the world with over 27,000 professionals who promote the game of golf to everyone.

There are about 32,000 golf courses in the world

There are over 15,000 golf courses in the United States

About 50 million people play golf.

The world's highest golf course is Tactu Golf Course, in the mountains of Peru, and is at an altitude of 14,335 feet above sea level

FUN QUIZ & PUZZLES

This is a fun quiz to help review all that you have learned. It's o.k. to use the book to look up any answers that you are not sure of.

1. The goal of golf is to

   a. play within the rules
   b. get the ball into the hole in as few strokes as possible
   c. play using good sportsmanship
   d. all of the above

2. Golf can be played with

   a. family and friends.
   b. raccoons.
   c. golf clubs.
   d. a and c.

3. The golf club that hits the ball the farthest is the

   a. putter.
   b. sand wedge.
   c. nine iron.
   d. driver.

4. The longest drivers can hit a golf ball

   a. 100 yards.
   b. 200 yards.
   c. 3000 yards.
   d. over 350 yards.

5. The game of golf has been around for

   a. 2 years.
   b. 20 years.
   c. 53 years.
   d. 600 years.

6. To play golf you will need golf clubs fit to your own

a. shoe size.
b. height.
c. shirt size.
d. favorite color.

7. Putting is rolling the ball on the

a. fairway.
b. rough.
c. bunker.
d. putting green.

8. You should always be__________ while others are playing.

a. quiet
b. still
c. out of the way
d. all of the above

9. You begin each hole from the

a. putting green.
b. fairway.
c. bunker.
d. teeing ground.

10. According to this book the most important fundamental when beginning to learn golf is the

a. set up position for each shot which includes proper posture, grip, alignment and ball position.
b. color of the golf ball you use.
c. name of your dog.
d. wearing of golf shoes or sneakers.

11. Which item is not included on a list of items to carry in your golf bag?

    a. Divot repair tool
    b. 12 golf balls
    c. Sunscreen
    d. A large, heavy, red brick

12. Proper dress attire means not wearing

    a. Flip-flops.
    b. soccer cleats.
    c. baseball cleats.
    d. all of the above.

13. Proper dress attire means wearing

    a. a collared golf shirt.
    b. sneakers or golf shoes.
    c. no denim pants or shorts.
    d. all of the above.

14. An example of good sportsmanship is

    a. shaking hands with other players after the game.
    b. being courteous during the round.
    c. helping others look for their lost golf balls.
    d. all of the above.

15. Hitting the driver require

    a. a wider stance than with irons.
    b. a full backswing and full balanced follow through.
    c. using a tee to tee the ball well above the ground.
    d. all of the above.

16. On a hot day while playing golf you should always

    a. wear a hat to protect from sunburn.
    b. wear sunscreen to protect from sunburn.
    c. drink plenty of water to stay hydrated.
    d. all of the above.

17. On a rainy day you can always

    a. practice your putting indoors.
    b. workout with weights to get stronger.
    c. learn about golf in magazines or online at golf websites.
    d. all of the above.

18. A golfer can carry up to________clubs in his bag.

    a. 8
    b. 10
    c. 33
    d. 14

19. A PGA Professional

    a. can give you golf lessons to get better.
    b. runs golf tournaments.
    c. runs the Pro Shop.
    d. all of the above.

20. The sand shot requires that you

    a. wiggle your feet into the sand and not let club head touch sand until you swing and hit behind the ball.
    b. make a full back swing and follow through.
    c. swing club head into sand before striking ball.
    d. all of the above.

21. The chip shot requires

    a. you lean your shaft slightly forward with hands in front of ball.
    b. you place your hands behind the ball.
    c. you try to roll the ball as much as possible once the ball lands on the green.
    d. both a and c.

22. Golfers can play in all types of weather except_________.

    a. cold.
    b. rain.
    c. windy.
    d. lightning.

23. Golfers must loudly yell_______to warn nearby golfers a ball is headed towards them.

 a. one.
 b. two.
 c. three.
 d. Fore!!

24. Good sportsmanship means being helpful to others on the course by

 a. being quiet, still and out of the way while they play their shots.
 b. helping others search for lost golf balls.
 c. putting the flagstick in after the last person putts out.
 d. all of the above.

25. Golf safety means

 a. making sure no one is near while you swing.
 b. not taking practice swings towards people.
 c. not hitting balls in the direction of people.
 d. all of the above.

26. The best way to get started for clubs is to buy a matched junior set according to your measured

 a. height.
 b. weight.
 c. shoe size.
 d. none of the above.

27. Who is the best-qualified professional to give you golf advice?

 a. Doctor
 b. Lawyer
 c. PGA Professional
 d. Race Car Driver

28. It is important to always identify and play your own golf ball by

 a. knowing the brand name of your ball.
 b. knowing the number on your ball.
 c. using a permanent marker to add your own unique art or

marking on the ball.

d. all of the above.

29. PGA of America is

a. an association of professional golfers.
b. a country in South America.
c. a time zone.
d. a television channel for golf.

30. When your ball goes out of bounds or is lost you must

a. look for your ball until you find it.
b. go home and have a chocolate milk shake.
c. get angry and upset.
d. replay another ball from where you hit it from with a one stroke penalty.

31. An eagle is a score that is

a. one over par.
b. two over par.
c. one under par.
d. two under par.

32. A birdie is a score that is

a. one over par.
b. two over par.
c. one under par.
d. two under par.

33. A bogey is a score that is

a. one over par.
b. two over par.
c. three over par.
d. one under par.

34. Par is a score that is

a. a good score.
b. a bad score.
c. neither over or under par.
d. both a and c.

35. Putting games on the practice green are both a fun way to compete and also a way to get better at putting.

a. True
b. False

36. You can mark your ball on the putting green with

a. a twig, small stick or a piece of grass.
b. a small round flat round object such as a coin.
c. a small rock.
d. a plastic army man.

37. A fade (for a right handed golfer) is a shot that curves in the air

a. slightly to the left.
b. a lot to the left.
c. slightly to the right.
d. goes very straight.

38. You may pick up loose objects on the green such as

a. insects.
b. leaves.
c. sticks.
d. all of the above.

39. A caddy helps and assists a player with

a. yardage to the hole and club selection.
b. hits the tough shots for the player.
c. carrying clubs and course care.
d. both a and c.

40. This book recommends that you practice your set up

a. in front of your dog.
b. in front of a window.
c. in front of your cat.
d. in front of a mirror.

41. When your ball is on a cart path you may

a. hit the ball off the cart path.
b. take relief from the cart path without penalty.

c. take your ball off the cart path with a one stroke penalty.
d. both a and b.

42. A water hazard has three options and is defined by

a. white stakes.
b. red stakes.
c. yellow stakes.
d. none of the above.

43. A lateral water hazard has five options and is defined by

a. white stakes.
b. red stakes.
c. yellow stakes.
d. none of the above.

44. Out of bounds is defined by

a. white stakes.
b. red stakes.
c. yellow stakes.
d. none of the above.

45. If your ball falls off a tee it doesn't count as a stroke and can be re-teed

a. True
b. False

46. You can clean your ball whenever taking relief

a. True
b. False

47. "Ready Golf" means playing your shot when you are ready and without endangering other players

a. True
b. False

48. To hit the ball far this book recommends practice swinging and producing a loud swish sound

a. True
b. False

49. The curving path of a putt is called

  a. the break.
  b. a slice.
  c. a draw.
  d. a fade.

50. Golf is a very________sport.

  a. difficult
  b. old
  c. fun
  d. all of the above

Answers to Fun Quiz

1d, 2d, 3d, 4d, 5d, 6b, 7d, 8d, 9d, 10a, 11d, 12d, 13d, 14d, 15d, 16d, 17d, 18d, 19d, 20d, 21d, 22d, 23d, 24d, 25d, 26a, 27c, 28d, 29a, 30d, 31d, 32c, 33a, 34d, 35a, 36b, 37c, 38d, 39d, 40d, 41d, 42c, 43b, 44a, 45a, 46a, 47a, 48a, 49a, 50d

Really hard word search puzzles

```
E B A F Q Y K Z Y P X J C B D
H A H B T S I E L T I T O M S
C M G Y A B C T R P H L Z E S
S U A L K C I N K C A J N L D
D T Y H E R K R N H M O I E O
W I W R E O T S R Y J C A G O
L S R K O V P O W Y E I D N W
L O C B R T F M B I N L U I R
D A T X Y W C B E I N A C R E
H J P B Z H O E N T A G K F G
D Y K O P B U E J X W S H P I
F L A G S T I C K A Z U O Z T
V H M E D R I V E R R F O I M
J N Q Y O E M M I G A T K Q J
M P S N Q G U Q T T F Z C T D
```

BOBBYJONES
BOGEY
DRIVER
DUCKHOOK
EAGLE
FLAGSTICK
FRINGE
GIMME
HACKER
JACKNICKLAUS
NINEIRON
SLICE
TEMPO
TIGERWOODS
TITLEIST
TRAJECTORY
USGA
BACKSWING
HYBRID
Bonus: LOB

```
R S E H X L E T R W S D N O E
D E S X I F R G O A Y F R R C
I H K N O A X R D C P P Q U A
V M K N C T M X X E A A X J T
O S U F U B N N C G W X E E T
T S L O U B V I P B A D E X F
N O Y R F L O P S H O T N J G
G I N I H N M S O S I E G A P
T E B C V H S K N M V I O L S
R L H L A F S C E G H D K A A
I M B C I D Q A P D R R P G E
I T W O V C D B U O Q I U L W
D O G L E G K Y T L O B C M B
Y A W R I A F J T Y D N A S W
R E H S A W L L A B T Z W U A
```

BACKSPIN	BALLWASHER
BIRDIE	BUNKER
CADDY	DIVOT
DOGLEG	FAIRWAY
FLOPSHOT	GOLFCART
LINKS	NIBLICK
ONEPUTT	PAR
PGAPRO	SANDWEDGE
SANDY	TEETIME
WORMBURNER	Bonus: ACE

ABOUT THE AUTHOR

An outstanding junior golfer in his home state of Massachusetts Jon competed successfully in many local, state and national junior golf tournaments. In recognition of his many achievements Jon was recently inducted into his high school's Sports Hall of Fame.

Upon graduating from high school in addition to receiving a golf scholarship to attend Rollins College in Winter Park, Florida where he was a member of the golf team, Jon was awarded a prestigious Francis Ouimet golf scholarship

Jon began his professional golf career as a PGA apprentice at Lake Nona CC in Orlando, Florida and earned his Class A PGA card in 1997.

Jon has a passion for teaching golf, and, especially for teaching golf to juniors. "Junior Golf in Pictures" is the result of his years of teaching experience, coaching experience and his love for the game. Jon currently resides with his wife and sons, Nick and Chris, in Smyrna, Georgia.

Jon's book of golf tips, "Play Better Golf", is available on amazon.com, Barnes & Noble, Smashwords, and iBooks.

Junior Golf In Pictures is also available as an eBook on amazon.com.

10_2_32d